Cram101 Textbook Outlines to accompany:

History of World Societies: Volume A

McKay, Patricia Buckley Ebrey, John Buckler, Roger B. Beck, Bennett Hill, 7th Edition

A Cram101 Inc. publication (c) 2010.

Cram101 Textbook Outlines and Cram101.com are Cram101 Inc. publications and services. All notes, highlights, reviews, and practice tests are written and prepared by Cram101, all rights reserved.

PRACTICE EXAMS.

Get all of the self-teaching practice exams for each chapter of this textbook at **www.Cram101.com** and ace the tests. Here is an example:

Chapter 1

History of World Societies: Volume A
McKay, Patricia Buckley Ebrey, John Buckler, Roger B. Beck, Bennett Hill, 7th Edition,
All Material Written and Prepared by Cram101

I WANT A BETTER GRADE.   Items 1 - 50 of 100.

1. _____ participated in World War I from 1914 to 1917, as one of the major Entente Powers and played an important role in securing the sea lanes in South Pacific and Indian Oceans against the Kaiserliche Marine. Politically, _____ seized the opportunity to expand its sphere of influence in China, and to gain recognition as a great power in postwar geopolitics.

   On 7 August 1914, the _____ese government received an official request from the British government for assistance in destroying the German raiders of the Kaiserliche Marine in and around Chinese waters.

   ○ Japan   ○ J. F. Lehmann
   ○ Jabal al-Druze   ○ Jackshaft

2. The great end, for which men entered into society, was to secure their property. That right is preserved sacred and incommunicable in all instances, where it has not been taken away or abridged by some public _____ for the good of the whole ... If no excuse can be found or produced, the silence of the books is an authority against the defendant, and the plaintiff must have judgment.

   ○ Law   ○ La France au travail
   ○ La Giovine Italia   ○ La Isabela

3. The term _____ commonly refers to a political or geographical domain such as the Ottoman Empire, the French Empire the Russian Empire, the Chinese Empire etc., but the term can equally be applied to domains of knowledge, beliefs, values and expertise, such as the empires of Christianity or Islam . _____ is usually autocratic, and also sometimes monolithic in character.

You get a 50% discount for the online exams. Go to **Cram101.com**, click Sign Up at the top of the screen, and enter DK73DW6916 in the promo code box on the registration screen. Access to Cram101.com is $4.95 per month, cancel at any time.

With Cram101.com online, you also have access to extensive reference material.

You will nail those essays and papers. Here is an example from a Cram101 Biology text:

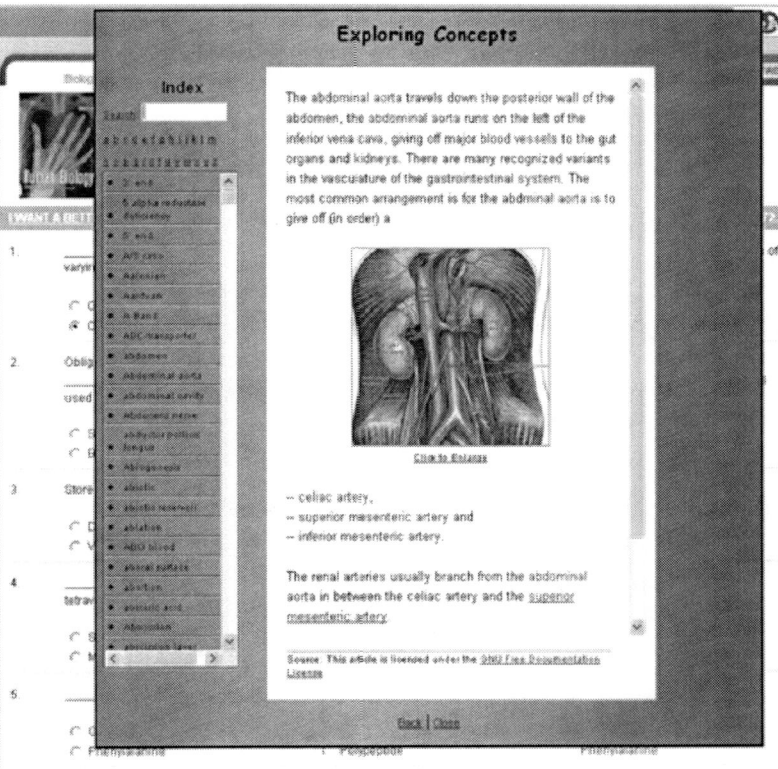

Visit **www.Cram101.com**, click Sign Up at the top of the screen, and enter DK73DW6916 in the promo code box on the registration screen. Access to www.Cram101.com is normally $9.95 per month, but because you have purchased this book, your access fee is only $4.95 per month, cancel at any time. Sign up and stop highlighting textbooks forever.

Learning System

Cram101 Textbook Outlines is a learning system. The notes in this book are the highlights of your textbook, you will never have to highlight a book again.

How to use this book. Take this book to class, it is your notebook for the lecture. The notes and highlights on the left hand side of the pages follow the outline and order of the textbook. All you have to do is follow along while your instructor presents the lecture. Circle the items emphasized in class and add other important information on the right side. With Cram101 Textbook Outlines you'll spend less time writing and more time listening. Learning becomes more efficient.

Cram101.com Online

Increase your studying efficiency by using Cram101.com's practice tests and online reference material. It is the perfect complement to Cram101 Textbook Outlines. Use self-teaching matching tests or simulate in-class testing with comprehensive multiple choice tests, or simply use Cram's true and false tests for quick review. Cram101.com even allows you to enter your in-class notes for an integrated studying format combining the textbook notes with your class notes.

Visit **www.Cram101.com**, click Sign Up at the top of the screen, and enter **DK73DW6916** in the promo code box on the registration screen. Access to www.Cram101.com is normally $9.95 per month, but because you have purchased this book, your access fee is only $4.95 per month. Sign up and stop highlighting textbooks forever.

Copyright © 2010 by Cram101, Inc. All rights reserved. "Cram101"® and "Never Highlight a Book Again!"® are registered trademarks of Cram101, Inc. ISBN(s): 9781616548773. EDE-5 .20091230

History of World Societies: Volume A
McKay, Patricia Buckley Ebrey, John Buckler, Roger B. Beck, Bennett Hill, 7th

CONTENTS

1. Early Civilizations 2
2. The Foundation of Indian Society, to 300C.E. 14
3. China`s Classical Age, to 256B.C.E. 22
4. The Greek Experience 24
5. The World of Rome 34
6. East Asia and the Spread of Buddhism, 256B.c.E.-800c.E. 46
7. The Making of Europe 52
8. The Islamic World, ca 600-1400 60
9. African Societies and Kingdoms, ca 400-1450 66
10. Central and Southern Asia, to 1400 72
11. East Asia, ca 800-1400 84
12. Europe in the Middle Ages 92
13. Civilizations of the Americas, ca 400-1500 106

Chapter 1. Early Civilizations

Japan	Japan participated in World War I from 1914 to 1917, as one of the major Entente Powers and played an important role in securing the sea lanes in South Pacific and Indian Oceans against the Kaiserliche Marine. Politically, Japan seized the opportunity to expand its sphere of influence in China, and to gain recognition as a great power in postwar geopolitics. On 7 August 1914, the Japanese government received an official request from the British government for assistance in destroying the German raiders of the Kaiserliche Marine in and around Chinese waters.
Law	The great end, for which men entered into society, was to secure their property. That right is preserved sacred and incommunicable in all instances, where it has not been taken away or abridged by some public Law for the good of the whole ... If no excuse can be found or produced, the silence of the books is an authority against the defendant, and the plaintiff must have judgment.
Imperialism	The term Imperialism commonly refers to a political or geographical domain such as the Ottoman Empire, the French Empire the Russian Empire, the Chinese Empire etc., but the term can equally be applied to domains of knowledge, beliefs, values and expertise, such as the empires of Christianity or Islam . Imperialism is usually autocratic, and also sometimes monolithic in character. Imperialism is found in the ancient histories of the Assyrian Empire, Chinese Empire, Roman Empire, Greece, the Persian Empire, and the Ottoman Empire , ancient Egypt, India, the Aztec empire, and a basic component to the conquests of Genghis Khan and other warlords.
Slavery	Slavery (Romanian: robie) existed on the territory of present-day Romania from before the founding of the principalities of Wallachia and Moldavia in 13th-14th century, until it was abolished in stages during the 1840s and 1850s. Most of the slaves were of Roma (Gypsy) ethnicity. Particularly in Moldavia there were also slaves of Tatar ethnicity, probably prisoners captured from the wars with the Nogai and Crimean Tatars.
Uruk	Uruk was an ancient city of Sumer and later Babylonia, situated east of the present bed of the Euphrates river, on the ancient dry former channel of the Euphrates River, some 30 km east of modern As-Samawah, Al-MuthannÄ , Iraq.
Babylonia	Babylonia was a state in Lower Mesopotamia (Iraq), with Babylon as its capital. Babylonia emerged when Hammurabi (fl. ca. 1696 - 1654 BC, short chronology) created an empire out of the territories of the former kingdoms of Sumer and Akkad. The Amorites being a Semitic people, Babylonia adopted the written Semitic Akkadian language for official use, and retained the Sumerian language for religious use, which by that time was no longer a spoken language.
Ecbatana	Ecbatana is supposed to be the capital of Astyages (Istuvegü), which was taken by the Persian emperor Cyrus the Great in the sixth year of Nabonidus . Under the Persian kings, Ecbatana, situated at the foot of Mount Alvand, became a summer residence. Later, it became the capital of the Parthian kings, at which time it became their main mint, producing drachm, tetradrachm, and assorted bronze denominations.

Chapter 1. Early Civilizations

Chapter 1. Early Civilizations

Empire — The term Empire derives from the Latin imperium. Politically, an Empire is a geographically extensive group of states and peoples united and ruled either by a monarch (emperor, empress) or an oligarchy. Geopolitically, the term Empire has denoted very different, territorially-extreme states -- at the strong end, the extensive Spanish Empire and the British Empire (19th c)., at the weak end, the Holy Roman Empire (8th c.-19th c)., in its Medieval and early-modern forms, and the Byzantine Empire (15th c)., that was a direct continuation of the Roman Empire, that, in its final century of existence, was more a city-state than a territorial Empire.

Syria — Syria operated under a federalist system during its period of French rule . Its constituents were organized on primarily ethno-religious lines: there were separate states for Maronites, Alawites, Druze and Turks. The federal system was abolished after the Syrian independence in 1946.

Tigris — The Tigris is the eastern member of the two great rivers that define Mesopotamia, along with the Euphrates, which flows from the mountains of southeastern Turkey through Iraq.
The original Sumerian name was Idigna or Idigina, probably from *id gina "running water", which can be interpreted as "the swift river", contrasted to its neighbor, the Euphrates, whose leisurely pace caused it to deposit more silt and build up a higher bed than the Tigris. This form was borrowed and gave rise to Akkadian Idiqlat.

New Kingdom — The New Kingdom sometimes referred to as the Egyptian Empire, is the period in ancient Egyptian history between the 16th century BC and the 11th century BC, covering the Eighteenth, Nineteenth, and Twentieth Dynasties of Egypt. The New Kingdom (1570-1070 BC) followed the Second Intermediate Period and was succeeded by the Third Intermediate Period. It was Egypt"s most prosperous time and marked the zenith of its power.

Peasant — A Peasant is an agricultural worker who subsists by working a small plot of ground. The term Peasant today is sometimes used in a pejorative sense for impoverished farmers.
Peasants typically make up the majority of the agricultural labour force in a Pre-industrial society, dependent on the cultivation of their land: without stockpiles of provisions they thrive or starve according to the most recent harvest.

Avaris — Avaris , was located near modern Tell el-Dab"a in the northeastern region of the Nile Delta. As the main course of the Nile migrated eastward and the delta sedimented up and moved with the river, its position at the hub of Egypt"s delta emporia made it a major administrative capital of the Hyksos and other traders. From c 1783-1550 BC or from the Thirteenth Dynasty of Egypt through the second intermediate until its destruction by Kamose brought to a close the Seventeenth dynasty, Avaris brought a little bit of Canaan home to Egypt.

Hattusa — Hattusa (URUá¸ªa-at-tu-Å¡a ô'Œ·ô',©ô'€œô'Œ...ô'Š; á¸ªattuÅ¡a, near modern BoÄŸazkale (formerly BoÄŸazköy), Turkey) was the capital of the Hittite Empire in the late Bronze Age. The region is set in a loop of the KÄ±zÄ±l River (Marashantiya in Hittite sources and Halys in Classical Antiquity) in central Anatolia.
Hattusa was added to the UNESCO World Heritage list in 1986.

Chapter 1. Early Civilizations

Kadesh

Kadesh (also Qadesh) was an ancient city of the Levant, located on or near the headwaters or ford of the Orontes River It is surmised by Kenneth Kitchen to be the ruins at Tell Nebi Mend, about 24 kilometers (15 mi) southwest of Homs (ca. 34°35′N 36°31′Eï»¿ / ï»¿34.583°N 36.517°E) near Al Qusayr in what is now western Syria but is located in the text of the inscriptions at the battle of Kadesh as near Tunip in the land of the Amurru. Kadesh was the target of military campaigns by most of the pharoahs of the Eighteenth dynasty of Egypt and one of many outlying vassals won by the southerly encroachments of the Hittite Empire between 1500 and 1285 BC. Between 1504 and 1492 BC Thutmosis I campaigned north into Syria against the Mitanni a vassal of the Hittites and along with Aram an ally of Kadesh. In 1479 BC Thutmoses III fought against the king of Kadesh in the Battle of Megiddo.

Byblos

Byblos (BÏ βλος) is the Greek name of the Phoenician city Gebal . It is a Mediterranean city in the Mount Lebanon Governorate of present-day Lebanon under the current Arabic name of Jbeil (Ø¬Ø¨ÙŠÙ„ Ç¦ubayl) and was also referred to as Gibelet during the Crusades. It is believed to have been founded around 5000 BC, and according to fragments attributed to the semi-legendary pre-Trojan war Phoenician historian Sanchuniathon, it was built by Cronus as the first city in Phoenicia.

Carthage

Carthage refers both to an ancient city in present-day Tunisia, and a modern-day suburb of Tunis. The civilization that developed within the city"s sphere of influence is referred to as Punic or Carthaginian. The city of Carthage is located on the eastern side of Lake Tunis across from the center of Tunis.

Ottoman

The state of the Ottomans which began as part of the Anatolian Seljuk Sultanate and became an independent Empire, has been known historically by different names at different periods and in various languages. This page surveys the history of these names and their usage.

· Modern Turkish: OsmanlÄ± BeyliÄŸi;
The first declaration of statehood happened under Osman I.

· Ä€l-e Uá'mÄ n

Chapter 1. Early Civilizations

Chapter 1. Early Civilizations

	· Medieval Latin: Turchia · Medieval Latin: Imperium Turcicum · English: Turkey ; the current use of the name Turkey refers to the Republic of Turkey which succeeded the Ottoman Empire in 1923 · English: Turkish Empire, Ottoman Empire, Osmanic Empire, Osmanian Empire · Ottoman Turkish/Persian: Ø¯ÙÙ„Øª Ø¹Ù„ÙŠÙ‡ Ø¹Ø«Ù…Ø§Ù†ÙŠÙ‡ Devlet-i Âliye-yi Osmâniyye · Ottoman Turkish/Persian: Devlet-i Âliye (The Sublime State) · Ottoman Turkish/Persian: Devlet-i Ebed-Müddet · Ottoman Turkish/Persian: Memâlik-i Mahrûse (The Well-Protected Domains) · Ottoman Turkish/Persian: Memâlik-i Mahrûse-i Osmanî · Modern Turkish: Osmanlı Ä°mparatorluÄŸu (Ottoman Empire), · Arabic: Ø§Ù„Ø¯ÙˆÙ„Ø© Ø§Ù„Ø¹Ù„ÙŠØ©ª Ø§Ù„Ø¹Ø«Ù…Ø§Ù†ÙŠØ©ª Ad-Dawlat al-ʤĀĺĬ« al-ʤUthmÄ nÄ« · Bulgarian: ÐžÑ Ð¼Ð°Ð½Ñ ÐºÐ° Ð˜Ð¼Ð¿ÐµÑ€Ð¸Ñ (Osmanska Imperia) · Greek: ΟθωμανικÎ® ΑυτοκρατορÎ"α · Armenian: Օ·Õ½Õ´Õ¡Õ¶ÕµÕ¡Õ¶ Օ¿Õ¡ÕµÕ½Ö€Õ¸Ö‚Õ©ÕµÕ¸Õ¶ (Osmanyan Kaysroutyoun) In diplomatic circles, the Ottoman government was often referred to as the "Sublime Porte", a literal translation of the Ottoman Turkish Bâb-ı Âlî, which was the only gate of the imperial Topkapı Palace that was open to foreigners, and where the Sultan, Grand Vizier or Viziers greeted the ambassadors.
Ottoman Empire	The Ottoman Empire or Ottoman State , also known by its contemporaries as the Turkish Empire or Turkey , was an empire that lasted from 1299 to November 1, 1922 (as an imperial monarchy) or July 24, 1923 (de jure, as a state.) It was succeeded by the Republic of Turkey, which was officially proclaimed on October 29, 1923. At the height of its power (16th-17th century), it spanned three continents, controlling much of Southeastern Europe, Western Asia and North Africa.
Rome	Rome is the capital of Italy and the country"s largest and most populous city, with over 2.7 million residents in a municipality of some 1,285.3 km^2 (496.3 sq mi), while the population of the urban area is estimated by Eurostat to be 3.46 million. The metropolitan area of Rome is estimated by OECD to have a population of 3.7 million. It is located in the central-western portion of the Italian Peninsula, on the Tiber river.
Sidon	Sidon or Saïda, is the third-largest city in Lebanon. It is located in the South Governorate of Lebanon, on the Mediterranean coast, about 40 km north of Tyre and 40 km (25 mi) south of the capital Beirut. Its name means a fishery.
Tyre	Tyre is a city in the South Governorate of Lebanon. There were approximately 117,000 inhabitants in 2003, however, the government of Lebanon has released only rough estimates of population numbers since 1932, so an accurate statistical accounting is not possible. Tyre juts out from the coast of the Mediterranean Sea and is located about 80 km south of Beirut.

Chapter 1. Early Civilizations

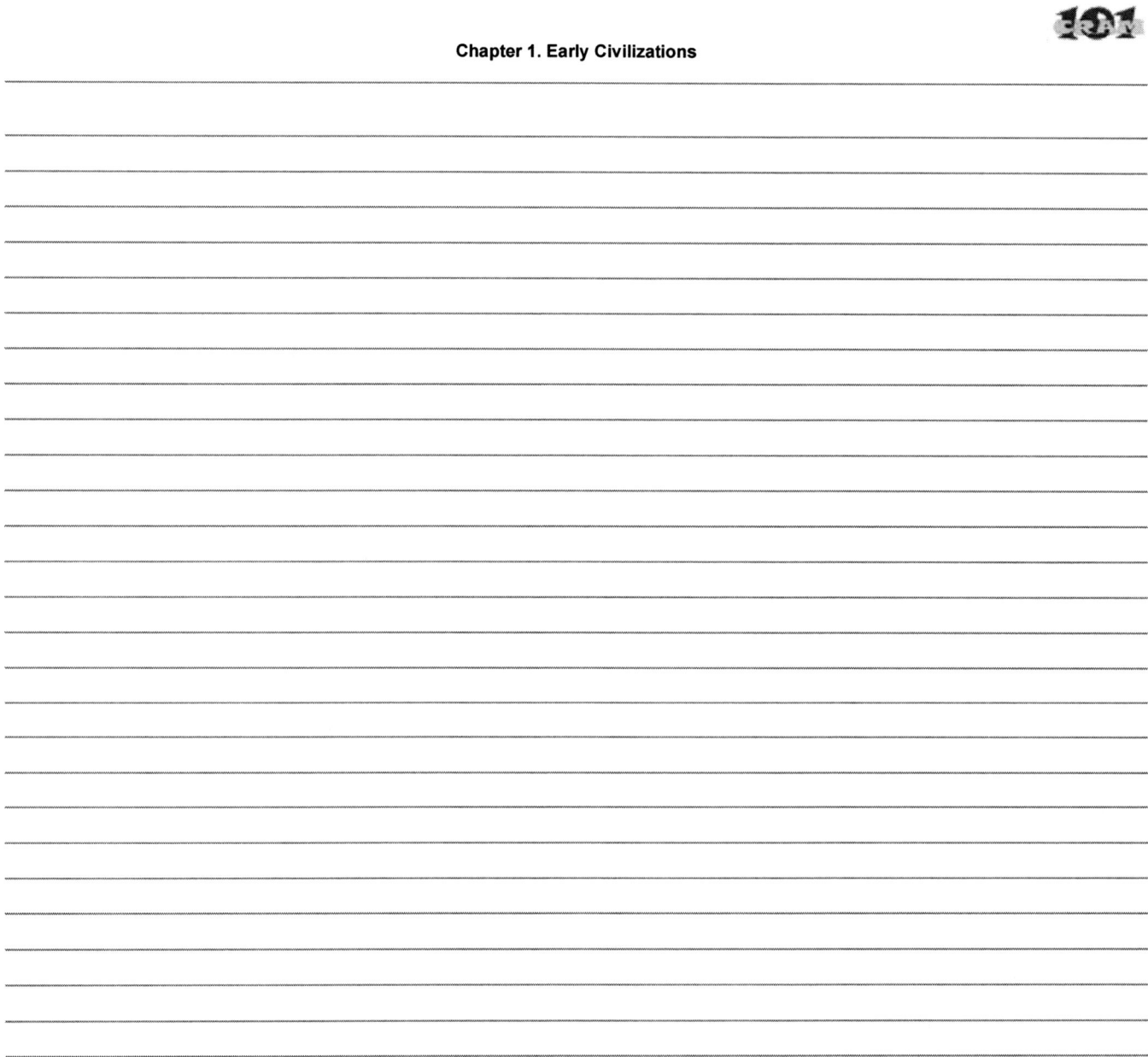

Chapter 1. Early Civilizations

Ashkelon	Ashkelon or Ashqelon ; Latin: Ascalon; Akkadian: Isqalluna) is a coastal city in the South District of Israel. The ancient seaport of Ashkelon dates back to the Bronze Age. In the course of its history, it has been ruled by the Canaanites, the Philistines, The Israelites, the Babylonians, the Greeks, the Phoenicians, the Romans, the Persians, the Egyptians, the Muslims, the British and the Crusaders.
France	France or ; French: [fÊ É'Ìʃs]), officially the French Republic , is a country located in Western Europe, with several overseas islands and territories located on other continents. Metropolitan France extends from the Mediterranean Sea to the English Channel and the North Sea, and from the Rhine to the Atlantic Ocean. It is often referred to as L"Hexagone ("The Hexagon") because of the geometric shape of its territory.
Ten Commandments	The Ten Commandments are a list of religious and moral imperatives that, according to Judeo-Christian tradition, were authored by God and given to Moses on the mountain referred to as "Mount Sinai" (Exodus 19:23) or "Horeb" (Deuteronomy 5:2) in the form of two stone tablets. They are recognized as a moral foundation in Judaism, Christianity and Islam. In Biblical Hebrew, the commandments are called ×¢×©×¨×ª ×"×"×'×"×™× and in Rabbinical Hebrew ×¢×©×¨×ª ×"×'×"×•×ª (transliterated Aseret ha-Dibrot), both translatable as "the ten terms." The English name "Decalogue" is derived from the Greek translation δεκÎ¬λογος dekalogos "ten terms", found in the Septuagint at Exodus 34:28 and Deuteronomy 10:4.
Capital	

	Flag

The three occupation zones. Blue indicates the Italian, red the German and green the Bulgarian zones. The Italian zone was taken over by the Germans in September 1943.

Capital	Athens
Political structure	Puppet state
Prime Minister	
- 1941-1942	Georgios Tsolakoglou
- 1942-1943	Konst.

Nineveh	Nineveh , an "exceeding great city", as it is called in the Book of Jonah, lay on the eastern bank of the Tigris in ancient Assyria, across the river from the modern-day major city of Mosul, Iraq. Ancient Nineveh s mound-ruins of Kouyunjik and NabÄ« YÅ«nus are located on a level part of the plain near the junction of the Tigris and the Khosr Rivers within an 1,800-acre area circumscribed by a 12-kilometre (7.5 mi) brick rampart. This whole extensive space is now one immense area of ruins overlaid in parts by new suburbs of the city of Mosul.
Medes	The Medes were an ancient Iranian people who lived in the northwestern portions of present-day Iran. This area is known as Media . They entered this region with the first wave of Iranian tribes, in the late second millennium BC (the Bronze Age collapse).
Parthia	Parthia is a region of north-eastern Iran, best known for having been the political and cultural base of the Arsacid dynasts, after which the Arsacid Empire is then also known as the "Parthian Empire".

Chapter 1. Early Civilizations

Chapter 1. Early Civilizations

	The name "Parthia" is a continuation from Latin Parthia, from Old Persian Parthava, which was the Parthian language self-designator signifying "of the Parthians".
	Parthia roughly corresponds to the western half of Khorasan.
Lydia	Lydia was an Iron Age kingdom of western Asia Minor located generally east of ancient Ionia in the modern Turkish provinces of Manisa and inland İzmir. Its population spoke an Anatolian language known as Lydian.
	At its greatest extent, the Kingdom of Lydia covered all of western Anatolia.
Mountain	A Mountain is a large landform that stretches above the surrounding land in a limited area usually in the form of a peak. A Mountain is generally steeper than a hill. The adjective montane is used to describe Mountainous areas and things associated with them.
Sardis	Sardis also Sardes, modern Sart in the Manisa province of Turkey, was the capital of the ancient kingdom of Lydia, one of the important cities of the Persian Empire, the seat of a proconsul under the Roman Empire, and the metropolis of the province Lydia in later Roman and Byzantine times. As one of the Seven churches of Asia, it was addressed by the author of the Book of Revelation in terms which seem to imply that its population was notoriously soft and fainthearted. Its importance was due, first to its military strength, secondly to its situation on an important highway leading from the interior to the Aegean coast, and thirdly to its commanding the wide and fertile plain of the Hermus.
Ephesus	Ephesus was an ancient Greek city on the west coast of Anatolia, near present-day Selçuk, Izmir Province, Turkey. It was one of the twelve cities of the Ionian League during the Classical Greek period.
	The city was famed for the Temple of Artemis, one of the Seven Wonders of the Ancient World.
Susa	Susa was an ancient city of the Elamite, Persian and Parthian empires of Iran, located about 250 km east of the Tigris River.
	The modern Iranian town of Shush is located at the site of ancient Susa
	Winged sphinx from the palace of Darius the Great at Susa
Roman	A Roman or civil diocese was one of the administrative divisions of the later Roman Empire, starting with the Tetrarchy. It formed the intermediate level of government, grouping several provinces and being in turn subordinated to a praetorian prefecture.
	The earliest use of "diocese" as an administrative unit was in the Greek-speaking East.

Chapter 2. The Foundation of Indian Society, to 300C.E.

Alexander	Alexander was tagus or despot of Pherae in Thessaly, and ruled from 369 BC to 358 BC. The accounts of his usurpation vary somewhat in minor points. Diodorus Siculus tells us that on the assassination of his father, the tyrant Jason of Pherae, in 370 BC, his brother Polydorus ruled for a year, and was then poisoned by Alexander, another brother. According to Xenophon, Polydorus was murdered by his brother Polyphron, and Polyphron, in 369 BC murdered by Alexander--his nephew, according to Plutarch, who relates also that Alexander worshiped the spear with which he slew his uncle as if it was a god.
Empire	The term Empire derives from the Latin imperium. Politically, an Empire is a geographically extensive group of states and peoples united and ruled either by a monarch (emperor, empress) or an oligarchy. Geopolitically, the term Empire has denoted very different, territorially-extreme states -- at the strong end, the extensive Spanish Empire and the British Empire (19th c)., at the weak end, the Holy Roman Empire (8th c.-19th c)., in its Medieval and early-modern forms, and the Byzantine Empire (15th c)., that was a direct continuation of the Roman Empire, that, in its final century of existence, was more a city-state than a territorial Empire.
India	India, officially the Indian Empire, declared war on Germany in September 1939. The Provinces of India " href="/wiki/East_African_Campaign_(World_War_II)">East African Campaign, Western Desert Campaign and the Italian Campaign. At the height of the World War, more than 2.5 million Indian troops were fighting Axis forces around the globe.
Mountain	A Mountain is a large landform that stretches above the surrounding land in a limited area usually in the form of a peak. A Mountain is generally steeper than a hill. The adjective montane is used to describe Mountainous areas and things associated with them.
Ethnicity	Ethnicity plays a prominent role in pornography. Distinct genres of pornography focus on performers of specific ethnic groups, or on the depiction of interracial sexual activity. Ethnic pornography typically employs ethnic and racial stereotypes in its depiction of performers.
Parthia	Parthia is a region of north-eastern Iran, best known for having been the political and cultural base of the Arsacid dynasts, after which the Arsacid Empire is then also known as the "Parthian Empire". The name "Parthia" is a continuation from Latin Parthia, from Old Persian Parthava, which was the Parthian language self-designator signifying "of the Parthians". Parthia roughly corresponds to the western half of Khorasan.
Nazi Germany	Nazi Germany and the Third Reich are the common English names for Germany between 1933 and 1945, while it was led by Adolf Hitler and the National Socialist German Worker"s Party . The name Third Reich (Drittes Reich, "Third Reich") refers to the state as the successor to the Holy Roman Empire of the Middle Ages and the German Empire of 1871-1918. In German, the state was known as Deutsches Reich until 1943, when its official name became Großdeutsches Reich .
Japan	Japan participated in World War I from 1914 to 1917, as one of the major Entente Powers and played an important role in securing the sea lanes in South Pacific and Indian Oceans against the Kaiserliche Marine. Politically, Japan seized the opportunity to expand its sphere of influence in China, and to gain recognition as a great power in postwar geopolitics.

Chapter 2. The Foundation of Indian Society, to 300C.E.

Chapter 2. The Foundation of Indian Society, to 300C.E.

On 7 August 1914, the Japanese government received an official request from the British government for assistance in destroying the German raiders of the Kaiserliche Marine in and around Chinese waters.

Ottoman

The state of the Ottomans which began as part of the Anatolian Seljuk Sultanate and became an independent Empire, has been known historically by different names at different periods and in various languages. This page surveys the history of these names and their usage.

· Modern Turkish: Osmanlı Beyliği;
The first declaration of statehood happened under Osman I.

· Āl-e Uá'mān

· Medieval Latin: Turchia
· Medieval Latin: Imperium Turcicum
· English: Turkey ; the current use of the name Turkey refers to the Republic of Turkey which succeeded the Ottoman Empire in 1923
· English: Turkish Empire, Ottoman Empire, Osmanic Empire, Osmanian Empire
· Ottoman Turkish/Persian: دولت علیه عثمانیه Devlet-i Âliye-yi Osmâniyye
· Ottoman Turkish/Persian: Devlet-i Âliye (The Sublime State)
· Ottoman Turkish/Persian: Devlet-i Ebed-Müddet
· Ottoman Turkish/Persian: Memâlik-i Mahrûse (The Well-Protected Domains)
· Ottoman Turkish/Persian: Memâlik-i Mahrûse-i Osmanî
· Modern Turkish: Osmanlı İmparatorluğu (Ottoman Empire),
· Arabic: الدولة العلية العثمانية Ad-Dawlat al-ʿAlīa al-ʿUthmānīa
· Bulgarian: Жъ Манскъ аа иманперъ, Ñ (Osmanska Imperia)
· Greek: Οθωμανική Αυτοκρατορία
· Armenian: Օսմանյան Կայսրություն (Osmanyan Kaysroutyoun)
In diplomatic circles, the Ottoman government was often referred to as the "Sublime Porte", a literal translation of the Ottoman Turkish Bâb-ı Âlî, which was the only gate of the imperial Topkapı Palace that was open to foreigners, and where the Sultan, Grand Vizier or Viziers greeted the ambassadors.

Ottoman Empire

The Ottoman Empire or Ottoman State , also known by its contemporaries as the Turkish Empire or Turkey , was an empire that lasted from 1299 to November 1, 1922 (as an imperial monarchy) or July 24, 1923 (de jure, as a state.) It was succeeded by the Republic of Turkey, which was officially proclaimed on October 29, 1923.
At the height of its power (16th-17th century), it spanned three continents, controlling much of Southeastern Europe, Western Asia and North Africa.

Chapter 2. The Foundation of Indian Society, to 300C.E.

Chapter 2. The Foundation of Indian Society, to 300C.E.

Slavery	Slavery (Romanian: robie) existed on the territory of present-day Romania from before the founding of the principalities of Wallachia and Moldavia in 13th-14th century, until it was abolished in stages during the 1840s and 1850s. Most of the slaves were of Roma (Gypsy) ethnicity. Particularly in Moldavia there were also slaves of Tatar ethnicity, probably prisoners captured from the wars with the Nogai and Crimean Tatars.
Rebellion	Rebellion is a refusal of obedience. It may, therefore, be seen as encompassing a range of behaviors from civil disobedience and mass nonviolent resistance, to violent and organized attempts to destroy an established authority such as the government. Those who participate in Rebellions are known as "rebels".
Magadha	Magadha formed one of the sixteen MahÄ janapadas or regions in ancient India. The core of the kingdom was the area of Bihar south of the Ganges; its first capital was Rajagaha (modern Rajgir) then Pataliputra (modern Patna). Magadha expanded to include most of Bihar and Bengal with the conquest of Licchavi and Anga respectively, followed by much of eastern Uttar Pradesh.
Nepal	Nepal (Nepali: à¤¨à¥‡à¤ªà¤¾à¤²), officially the Federal Democratic Republic of Nepal, is a landlocked country in South Asia and the world"s youngest republic. It is bordered to the north by the People"s Republic of China, and to the south, east, and west by the Republic of India. With an area of 147,181 square kilometres (56,827 sq mi) and a population of approximately 30 million, Nepal is the world"s 93rd largest country by land mass and the 41st most populous country.
Western world	The Western world is a term that can have multiple meanings depending on its context . Accordingly, the basic definition of what constitutes "the West" varies, expanding and contracting over time, in relation to various historical circumstances. Some historians believe the West originated in the northern and eastern Mediterranean with ancient Greece and ancient Rome.
Kushan empire	The Kushan Empire (c. 1st-3rd centuries CE) was originally formed in the territories of ancient Bactria on either side of the middle course of the Oxus River or Amu Darya in what is now northern Afghanistan, and southern Tajikistan and Uzbekistan. During the 1st and early 2nd centuries CE the Kushans expanded rapidly across the northern part of the Indian subcontinent at least as far as Sarnath near Varanasi (Benares) where inscriptions have been found dated to the first few years of era of the most famous Kushan ruler, Kanishka which apparently began about 127 CE. The Chinese history, the Hou Hanshu, gives an account of the formation of the Kushan Empire based on a report made by the Chinese general Ban Yong to the Chinese Emperor c.
Kozhikode	Kozhikode is a city in the southern Indian state of Kerala. It is the third largest city in Kerala and the headquarters of Kozhikode district. During the Middle Ages, Calicut was dubbed the "City of Spices" for its role as the major trading point of eastern spices.
Roman	A Roman or civil diocese was one of the administrative divisions of the later Roman Empire, starting with the Tetrarchy. It formed the intermediate level of government, grouping several provinces and being in turn subordinated to a praetorian prefecture.

Chapter 2. The Foundation of Indian Society, to 300C.E.

The earliest use of "diocese" as an administrative unit was in the Greek-speaking East.

Chapter 2. The Foundation of Indian Society, to 300C.E.

Chapter 3. China's Classical Age, to 256B.C.E.

India	India, officially the Indian Empire, declared war on Germany in September 1939. The Provinces of India " href="/wiki/East_African_Campaign_(World_War_II)">East African Campaign, Western Desert Campaign and the Italian Campaign. At the height of the World War, more than 2.5 million Indian troops were fighting Axis forces around the globe.
Liberal Union	The Liberal Union (in Dutch: Liberale Unie) was a Dutch liberal political party. A major party in its time, the Liberal Union was one of the historic predecessors of the Liberal State Party, and therefore of the People"s Party for Freedom and Democracy. Liberals had been an important political force in the Netherlands.
Aristocracy	Aristocracy is a form of government, in which a select few such as the most wise, strong or contributing citizens rule, often starting as a system of co-option where a council of prominent citizens add leading soldiers, merchants, land owners, priests, or lawyers to their number. Aristocracy deforms when it becomes hereditary elite. Aristocracies have most often been deformed to hereditary plutocratic systems.
Politics	Politics is a process by which groups of people make decisions. The term is generally applied to behavior within civil governments, but Politics has been observed in all human group interactions, including corporate, academic and religious institutions. It consists of "social relations involving authority or power" and refers to the regulation of a political unit, and to the methods and tactics used to formulate and apply policy.
Crossbow	A crossbow is a weapon consisting of a bow mounted on a stock that shoots projectiles, often called bolts. The medieval crossbow was called by many names, most of which derived from the word ballista, a siege engine resembling a crossbow in mechanism and appearance. crossbows historically played a significant role in the warfare of Europe, the Mediterranean, and Asia.
Roman	A Roman or civil diocese was one of the administrative divisions of the later Roman Empire, starting with the Tetrarchy. It formed the intermediate level of government, grouping several provinces and being in turn subordinated to a praetorian prefecture. The earliest use of "diocese" as an administrative unit was in the Greek-speaking East.
Qin Dynasty	The Qin Dynasty was the ruling Chinese dynasty between 221 and 206 BC. The Qin state was so named because its rulers were descendants of the first emperor"s ancestors whose fief was called "Qin". The Qin"s strength had been consolidated by Lord Shang Yang during the Warring States Period, in the 4th century BC. In the early third century BC, the Qin accomplished a series of swift conquests; the state subjugated the Chu, remnants of the Zhou Dynasty, and various other states to gain undisputed control of China. During its reign over China, the Qin Dynasty enjoyed increased trade, agriculture, and military security.

Chapter 3. China's Classical Age, to 256 B.C.E.

Chapter 4. The Greek Experience

Alexander	Alexander was tagus or despot of Pherae in Thessaly, and ruled from 369 BC to 358 BC.
	The accounts of his usurpation vary somewhat in minor points. Diodorus Siculus tells us that on the assassination of his father, the tyrant Jason of Pherae, in 370 BC, his brother Polydorus ruled for a year, and was then poisoned by Alexander, another brother. According to Xenophon, Polydorus was murdered by his brother Polyphron, and Polyphron, in 369 BC murdered by Alexander--his nephew, according to Plutarch, who relates also that Alexander worshiped the spear with which he slew his uncle as if it was a god.
Greece	Greece entered World War II on 28 October 1940, when the Italian army invaded from Albania. The Greek army dealt the first victory for the Allies by defeating the invasion and pushing Mussolini"s forces back into Albania. Hitler was reluctantly forced to send his own forces to overcome Greece in April 1941, and delay the invasion of the Soviet Union by six weeks.
India	India, officially the Indian Empire, declared war on Germany in September 1939. The Provinces of India " href="/wiki/East_African_Campaign_(World_War_II)">East African Campaign, Western Desert Campaign and the Italian Campaign. At the height of the World War, more than 2.5 million Indian troops were fighting Axis forces around the globe.
Ancient Greece	The term ancient Greece refers to the period of Greek history lasting from the Greek Dark Ages ca. 1100 BC and the Dorian invasion, to 146 BC and the Roman conquest of Greece after the Battle of Corinth. It is generally considered to be the seminal culture which provided the foundation of Western civilization and shaped cultures throughout Southwest Asia and North Africa. Greek culture had a powerful influence on the Roman Empire, which carried a version of it to many parts of the Mediterranean region and Europe. The civilization of the ancient Greeks has been immensely influential on language, politics, educational systems, philosophy, science, and the arts, inspiring the Islamic Golden Age and the Western European Renaissance, and again resurgent during various neo-Classical revivals in 18th and 19th century Europe and the Americas.
Argos	Argos is a city in Greece in the Peloponnese near Nafplion, which was its historic harbour " href="/wiki/Nauplius_(mythology)">Nauplius).
	The region of Argos is known as the Argolis, Argolid, or Argeia. The inhabitants of Argos were known as á¼"ργεá¿–οι or ArgÄ«vÄ« in Latin, rendered Argives in English.
Aristocracy	Aristocracy is a form of government, in which a select few such as the most wise, strong or contributing citizens rule, often starting as a system of co-option where a council of prominent citizens add leading soldiers, merchants, land owners, priests, or lawyers to their number. Aristocracy deforms when it becomes hereditary elite.
	Aristocracies have most often been deformed to hereditary plutocratic systems.
Hoplite	A Hoplite was a citizen-soldier of the Ancient Greek City-states. They were primarily armed as spear-men and fought in a phalanx formation. The word Hoplite derives from hoplon (á½…πλον, plural hopla á½…πλα), the type of the shield used by the troopers, although as a word "hoplon" could also denote weapons held or even full armament.

Chapter 4. The Greek Experience

Chapter 4. The Greek Experience

Force	In physics, a Force is any external agent that causes a change in the motion of a free body, or that causes stress in a fixed body. It can also be described by intuitive concepts such as a push or pull that can cause an object with mass to change its velocity , i.e., to accelerate, or which can cause a flexible object to deform. Force has both magnitude and direction, making it a vector quantity.
Carthage	Carthage refers both to an ancient city in present-day Tunisia, and a modern-day suburb of Tunis. The civilization that developed within the city"s sphere of influence is referred to as Punic or Carthaginian. The city of Carthage is located on the eastern side of Lake Tunis across from the center of Tunis.
Colonization	Colonization, , occurs whenever any one or more species populate an area. The term, which is derived from the Latin colere, "to inhabit, cultivate, frequent, practice, tend, guard, respect," originally related to humans. However, 19th century biogeographers dominated the term to describe the activities of birds, bacteria, or plant species.
Sparta	Sparta was an important Greek city-state in the Peloponnesus. It was unusual among Greek city-states in that it maintained its kingship past the Archaic age. It was even more unusual in that it had two kings simultaneously, coming from two separate lines.
Athens	Athens , the capital and largest city of Greece, dominates the Attica periphery; as one of the world"s oldest cities, its recorded history spans around 3,400 years. The Greek capital has a population of 745,514 within its administrative limits and a land area of 39 km^2 (15 sq mi). The urban area of Athens extends beyond the administrative city limits with a population of 3,130,841 (in 2001) and a land area of 412 km^2 (159 sq mi).
Cleisthenes	Cleisthenes was a noble Athenian of the Alcmaeonid family. He is credited with reforming the constitution of ancient Athens and setting it on a democratic footing in 508 BC or 507 BC. For these accomplishments, historians refer to him as "the father of Athenian democracy." He was the maternal grandson of the tyrant Cleisthenes of Sicyon, as the younger son of the latter"s daughter Agariste and her husband Megacles. According to William Smith, Cleisthenes was the maternal grandfather of Alcibiades.
Koinon	The Koinon (or "League") of Free Laconians was established in 21 BC by the Emperor Augustus, giving formal structure to a group of cities that had been associated for almost two centuries. The Eleutherolakones (á¼"λευθερολÎ¬κωνες, free Laconians) are first mentioned in 195 BC, after Sparta"s defeat in the Roman-Spartan War. The Roman general Titus Quinctius Flaminius placed several coastal cities of the Mani Peninsula under the protection of the Achean League, freeing them from Spartan hegemony.
Western world	The Western world is a term that can have multiple meanings depending on its context . Accordingly, the basic definition of what constitutes "the West" varies, expanding and contracting over time, in relation to various historical circumstances. Some historians believe the West originated in the northern and eastern Mediterranean with ancient Greece and ancient Rome.

Chapter 4. The Greek Experience

Chapter 4. The Greek Experience

Antigone	Antigone is the name of two different women in Greek mythology. The name may be taken to mean "unbending", coming from "anti-" and "-gon / -gony" (corner, bend, angle; ex: polygon), but has also been suggested to mean "opposed to motherhood" or "in place of a mother" based from the root gonÄ", "that which generates" .
Slavery	Slavery (Romanian: robie) existed on the territory of present-day Romania from before the founding of the principalities of Wallachia and Moldavia in 13th-14th century, until it was abolished in stages during the 1840s and 1850s. Most of the slaves were of Roma (Gypsy) ethnicity. Particularly in Moldavia there were also slaves of Tatar ethnicity, probably prisoners captured from the wars with the Nogai and Crimean Tatars.
Law	The great end, for which men entered into society, was to secure their property. That right is preserved sacred and incommunicable in all instances, where it has not been taken away or abridged by some public Law for the good of the whole ... If no excuse can be found or produced, the silence of the books is an authority against the defendant, and the plaintiff must have judgment.
Babylonia	Babylonia was a state in Lower Mesopotamia (Iraq), with Babylon as its capital. Babylonia emerged when Hammurabi (fl. ca. 1696 - 1654 BC, short chronology) created an empire out of the territories of the former kingdoms of Sumer and Akkad. The Amorites being a Semitic people, Babylonia adopted the written Semitic Akkadian language for official use, and retained the Sumerian language for religious use, which by that time was no longer a spoken language.
Boeotia	Boeotia, also spelled Beotia and BÅ"otia , formerly Cadmeis, was a region of ancient Greece, north of the eastern part of the Gulf of Corinth. It was bounded on the south by Megaris and the Kithairon mountain range that forms a natural barrier with Attica, on the north by Opuntian Locris and the Euripus Strait at the Gulf of Euboea, and on the west by Phocis. Lake Copais was a large lake in the center of Boeotia.
Delphi	Delphi is both an archaeological site and a modern town in Greece on the south-western spur of Mount Parnassus in the valley of Phocis. Delphi was the site of the Delphic oracle, the most important oracle in the classical Greek world, when it was a major site for the worship of the god Apollo after he slew the Python, a deity who lived there and protected the navel of the Earth. His sacred precinct in Delphi was a panhellenic sanctuary, where every four years athletes from all over the Greek world competed in the Pythian Games, one of the four panhellenic games, precursors to the Modern Olympics.
Politics	Politics is a process by which groups of people make decisions. The term is generally applied to behavior within civil governments, but Politics has been observed in all human group interactions, including corporate, academic and religious institutions. It consists of "social relations involving authority or power" and refers to the regulation of a political unit, and to the methods and tactics used to formulate and apply policy.

Chapter 4. The Greek Experience

Chapter 4. The Greek Experience

Republic	A Republic is a form of government in which the head of state is not a monarch and the people (or at least a part of its people) have an impact on its government. The word "Republic" is derived from the Latin phrase res publica which can be translated as "public affairs". Both modern and ancient Republics vary widely in their ideology and composition.
Epaminondas	Epaminondas was a Theban general and statesman of the 4th century BC who transformed the Ancient Greek city-state of Thebes, leading it out of Spartan subjugation into a preeminent position in Greek politics. In the process he broke Spartan military power with his victory at Leuctra and liberated the Messenian helots, a group of Peloponnesian Greeks who had been enslaved under Spartan rule for some 200 years. Epaminondas reshaped the political map of Greece, fragmented old alliances, created new ones, and supervised the construction of entire cities.
Thebes	
Corinth	Corinth, or Korinth is a city in Greece. In antiquity it was a city-state, on the Isthmus of Corinth, the narrow stretch of land that joins the Peloponnesus to the mainland of Greece. To the west of the isthmus lies the Gulf of Corinth, to the east lies the Saronic Gulf.
Susa	Susa was an ancient city of the Elamite, Persian and Parthian empires of Iran, located about 250 km east of the Tigris River. The modern Iranian town of Shush is located at the site of ancient Susa Winged sphinx from the palace of Darius the Great at Susa
Empire	The term Empire derives from the Latin imperium. Politically, an Empire is a geographically extensive group of states and peoples united and ruled either by a monarch (emperor, empress) or an oligarchy. Geopolitically, the term Empire has denoted very different, territorially-extreme states -- at the strong end, the extensive Spanish Empire and the British Empire (19th c.), at the weak end, the Holy Roman Empire (8th c.-19th c.), in its Medieval and early-modern forms, and the Byzantine Empire (15th c.), that was a direct continuation of the Roman Empire, that, in its final century of existence, was more a city-state than a territorial Empire.
Rome	Rome is the capital of Italy and the country"s largest and most populous city, with over 2.7 million residents in a municipality of some 1,285.3 km^2 (496.3 sq mi), while the population of the urban area is estimated by Eurostat to be 3.46 million. The metropolitan area of Rome is estimated by OECD to have a population of 3.7 million. It is located in the central-western portion of the Italian Peninsula, on the Tiber river.

Chapter 4. The Greek Experience

Chapter 4. The Greek Experience

France	France or ; French: [fÈ É˙ɟs]), officially the French Republic , is a country located in Western Europe, with several overseas islands and territories located on other continents. Metropolitan France extends from the Mediterranean Sea to the English Channel and the North Sea, and from the Rhine to the Atlantic Ocean. It is often referred to as L"Hexagone ("The Hexagon") because of the geometric shape of its territory.
Inca Empire	The Inca Empire (or Inka Empire) was the largest empire in pre-Columbian America. The administrative, political and military center of the empire was located in Cusco in modern-day Peru. The Inca Empire arose from the highlands of Peru sometime in early 13th century. From 1438 to 1533, the Incas used a variety of methods, from conquest to peaceful assimilation, to incorporate a large portion of western South America, centered on the Andean mountain ranges, including large parts of modern Ecuador, Peru, western and south central Bolivia, northwest Argentina, north and north-central Chile, and southern Colombia.

Chapter 4. The Greek Experience

Chapter 5. The World of Rome

Polybius	Polybius was a Greek historian of the Hellenistic Period noted for his book called The Histories covering in detail the period of 220-146 BC. He is also renowned for his ideas of political balance in government, which were later used in Montesquieu"s The Spirit of the Laws and in the drafting of the United States Constitution. Polybius was born around 203 BC in Megalopolis, Arcadia which at that time was an active member of the Achaean League. His father Lycortas was a prominent landowning politician and member of the governing class.
Roman	A Roman or civil diocese was one of the administrative divisions of the later Roman Empire, starting with the Tetrarchy. It formed the intermediate level of government, grouping several provinces and being in turn subordinated to a praetorian prefecture. The earliest use of "diocese" as an administrative unit was in the Greek-speaking East.
Rome	Rome is the capital of Italy and the country"s largest and most populous city, with over 2.7 million residents in a municipality of some 1,285.3 km^2 (496.3 sq mi), while the population of the urban area is estimated by Eurostat to be 3.46 million. The metropolitan area of Rome is estimated by OECD to have a population of 3.7 million. It is located in the central-western portion of the Italian Peninsula, on the Tiber river.
Italy	Italy (Italian: Italia), officially the Italian Republic (Italian: Repubblica Italiana), is a country located on the Italian Peninsula in Southern Europe and on the two largest islands in the Mediterranean Sea, Sicily and Sardinia. Italy shares its northern, Alpine boundary with France, Switzerland, Austria and Slovenia. The independent states of San Marino and the Vatican City are enclaves within the Italian Peninsula, and Campione d"Italia is an Italian exclave in Switzerland.
Mountain	A Mountain is a large landform that stretches above the surrounding land in a limited area usually in the form of a peak. A Mountain is generally steeper than a hill. The adjective montane is used to describe Mountainous areas and things associated with them.
Roman senate	Constitution of the Kingdom Constitution of the Republic Constitution of the Empire Constitution of the Late Empire History of the Constitution Senate Legislative Assemblies Executive Magistrates

Ordinary Magistrates
Extraordinary Magistrates
Titles and Honours
Emperor
Precedent and Law

Other countries Â· Atlas
Politics portal

Chapter 5. The World of Rome

Chapter 5. The World of Rome

Senate	The Roman Senate was a political institution in Ancient Rome. It was one of the most enduring institutions in Roman history, being founded before the first king of Rome ascended the throne (traditionally dated to 753 BC.) It survived the fall of the Roman Kingdom in 509 BC, the fall of the Roman Republic in 27 BC, and the fall of the Western Roman Empire in 476 AD. During the days of the kingdom, it was little more than an advisory council to the king. The Senate was the upper house of the Parliament of South Africa between 1910 and 1981, and between 1994 and 1997. Under white minority rule in the Union of South Africa, most of the Senators were chosen by an electoral college consisting of Members of each of the four Provincial Councils and Members of the House of Assembly (the lower house of Parliament, directly elected). The remaining Senators were appointed by the Governor General of the Union on the advice of the Prime Minister.
Empire	The term Empire derives from the Latin imperium. Politically, an Empire is a geographically extensive group of states and peoples united and ruled either by a monarch (emperor, empress) or an oligarchy. Geopolitically, the term Empire has denoted very different, territorially-extreme states -- at the strong end, the extensive Spanish Empire and the British Empire (19th c)., at the weak end, the Holy Roman Empire (8th c.-19th c)., in its Medieval and early-modern forms, and the Byzantine Empire (15th c)., that was a direct continuation of the Roman Empire, that, in its final century of existence, was more a city-state than a territorial Empire.
Roman Empire	The Roman Empire was the post-Republican phase of the ancient Roman civilization, characterised by an autocratic form of government and large territorial holdings in Europe and around the Mediterranean. The term is used to describe the Roman state during and after the time of the first emperor, Augustus. The nearly 500-year-old Roman Republic, which preceded it, had been weakened by several civil wars.
Western Roman Empire	The Western Roman Empire refers to the western half of the Roman Empire, from its division by Diocletian in 285; the other half of the Roman Empire was the Eastern Roman Empire, today widely known as the Byzantine Empire. The Western Empire existed intermittently in several periods between the 3rd century and 5th century, after Diocletian"s Tetrarchy and the reunifications associated with Constantine the Great and Julian the Apostate (324-363.) Theodosius I (379-395) was the last Roman Emperor who ruled over a unified Roman empire.
Law	The great end, for which men entered into society, was to secure their property. That right is preserved sacred and incommunicable in all instances, where it has not been taken away or abridged by some public Law for the good of the whole ... If no excuse can be found or produced, the silence of the books is an authority against the defendant, and the plaintiff must have judgment.
Carthage	Carthage refers both to an ancient city in present-day Tunisia, and a modern-day suburb of Tunis. The civilization that developed within the city"s sphere of influence is referred to as Punic or Carthaginian. The city of Carthage is located on the eastern side of Lake Tunis across from the center of Tunis.

Chapter 5. The World of Rome

Chapter 5. The World of Rome

Mare nostrum

Mare Nostrum was a Roman name for the Mediterranean Sea. In the years following the unification of Italy in 1861, the term was revived by Italian nationalists who believed that Italy was the successor state to the Roman Empire, and should seek to control ex-Roman territories in the Mediterranean. The term was again used by Benito Mussolini for use in fascist propaganda, in a similar manner to Adolf Hitler"s lebensraum.

Slavery

Slavery (Romanian: robie) existed on the territory of present-day Romania from before the founding of the principalities of Wallachia and Moldavia in 13th-14th century, until it was abolished in stages during the 1840s and 1850s. Most of the slaves were of Roma (Gypsy) ethnicity. Particularly in Moldavia there were also slaves of Tatar ethnicity, probably prisoners captured from the wars with the Nogai and Crimean Tatars.

Latifundia

Latifundia are pieces of property covering tremendous areas. The Latifundia of Roman history were great landed estates, specializing in agriculture destined for export: grain, olive oil, or wine. They were characteristic of Magna Graecia and Sicily, of Egypt and the North African Maghreb and of Hispania Baetica in southern Spain.

Republic

A Republic is a form of government in which the head of state is not a monarch and the people (or at least a part of its people) have an impact on its government. The word "Republic" is derived from the Latin phrase res publica which can be translated as "public affairs".
Both modern and ancient Republics vary widely in their ideology and composition.

First Triumvirate

The First Triumvirate was the political alliance of Gaius Julius Caesar, Marcus Licinius Crassus, and Gnaeus Pompeius Magnus. Unlike the Second Triumvirate, the First Triumvirate had no official status whatsoever - its overwhelming power in the Roman Republic was strictly unofficial influence, and was in fact kept secret for some time as part of the political machinations of the Triumvirates themselves. It was formed in 60 BC and lasted until Crassus"s death in 53 BC.
Crassus and Pompey had been colleagues in the consulate in 70 BC, when they had legislated the full restoration of the tribunate of the people .

Second Triumvirate

The Second Triumvirate is the name historians give to the official political alliance of Gaius Julius Caesar Octavianus (later known as Augustus), Marcus Aerulius Lepidus, and Mark Antony, formed on 26 November 43 BC with the enactment of the Lex Titia, the adoption of which marked the end of the Roman Republic. The Triumvirate existed for two five-year terms, covering the period 43 BC - 33 BC. Unlike the earlier First Triumvirate, the Second Triumvirate was an official, legally established institution, whose overwhelming power in the Roman state was given full legal sanction and whose imperium maius outranked that of all other magistrates, including the consuls.
The Triumvirate was legally established in 43 BC as the Triumviri Rei Publicae Constituendae Consulari Potestate .

Chapter 5. The World of Rome

Chapter 5. The World of Rome

Austria	Austria), officially the Republic of Austria , is a landlocked country of roughly 8.3 million people in Central Europe. It borders both Germany and the Czech Republic to the north, Slovakia and Hungary to the east, Slovenia and Italy to the south, and Switzerland and Liechtenstein to the west. The territory of Austria covers 83,872 square kilometres (32,383 sq mi), and is influenced by a temperate and alpine climate.
Princeps	Princeps (plural: principes) is a Latin word meanining "first in time or order; the first, chief, the most eminent, distinguished, or noble; the first man, first person" This article is devoted to a number of specific historical meanings the word took, the most important of which follows first. Princeps was an official title of a Roman Emperor, by some historians seen as the title determining the Emperor in Ancient Rome. The word "Princeps" derived from Princeps Senatus ("Primus inter pares" of the Senate).
Serbia	Serbia (Serbian: СрбиÑ˜Ð°, Srbija), officially the Republic of Serbia (Serbian: Ð Ðµпублика СрбиÑ˜Ð°, Republika Srbija), is a country located in both Central and Southeastern Europe. Its territory covers the southern part of the Pannonian Plain and central part of the Balkans. Serbia borders Hungary to the north; Romania and Bulgaria to the east; the Republic of Macedonia to the south; and Croatia, Bosnia and Herzegovina and Montenegro to the west.
Pompeii	Pompeii is a ruined and partially buried Roman town-city near modern Naples in the Italian region of Campania, in the territory of the comune of Pompei. Along with Herculaneum, its sister city, Pompeii was destroyed, and completely buried, during a long catastrophic eruption of the volcano Mount Vesuvius spanning two days in AD 79. The volcano collapsed higher roof-lines and buried Pompeii under 60 feet of ash and pumice, and it was lost for nearly 1,700 years before its accidental rediscovery in 1748.
Five good emperors	The Nervan-Antonian dynasty is a dynasty of seven consecutive Roman Emperors, who ruled over the Roman Empire from 96 to 192. These Emperors are Nerva, Trajan, Hadrian, Antoninus Pius, Marcus Aurelius, Lucius Verus and Commodus. Since the first five rulers - from Nerva to Marcus Aurelius are also seen as representing a line of virtuous and just rule, they also have been dubbed the Five Good Emperors.
Golden Age	The Golden Age is the term used to denote the historical period in Ancient Greece lasting roughly from the end of the Persian Wars in 448 BC to either the death of Pericles 429 BC or the end of the Peloponnesian War in 404 BC. Pericles - an Athenian general, politician, and orator - distinguished himself above the other shining personalities of the era, men who excelled in politics, philosophy, architecture, sculpture, history and literature. He fostered arts and literature and gave to Athens a splendor which would never return throughout its history. He executed a large number of public works projects and improved the life of the citizens.

Chapter 5. The World of Rome

Chapter 5. The World of Rome

India	India, officially the Indian Empire, declared war on Germany in September 1939. The Provinces of India " href="/wiki/East_African_Campaign_(World_War_II)">East African Campaign, Western Desert Campaign and the Italian Campaign. At the height of the World War, more than 2.5 million Indian troops were fighting Axis forces around the globe.
Plutarch	Plutarch was a tyrant of Eretria in Euboea. Whether he was the immediate successor of Themison, and also whether he was in any way connected with him by blood, are points which we have no means of ascertaining. Trusting perhaps to the influence of his friend Meidias, he applied to the Athenians in 354 BC for aid against his rival, Callias of Chalcis, who had allied himself with Philip of Macedon.
Athens	Athens , the capital and largest city of Greece, dominates the Attica periphery; as one of the world"s oldest cities, its recorded history spans around 3,400 years. The Greek capital has a population of 745,514 within its administrative limits and a land area of 39 km^2 (15 sq mi). The urban area of Athens extends beyond the administrative city limits with a population of 3,130,841 (in 2001) and a land area of 412 km^2 (159 sq mi).
Parthia	Parthia is a region of north-eastern Iran, best known for having been the political and cultural base of the Arsacid dynasts, after which the Arsacid Empire is then also known as the "Parthian Empire". The name "Parthia" is a continuation from Latin Parthia, from Old Persian Parthava, which was the Parthian language self-designator signifying "of the Parthians". Parthia roughly corresponds to the western half of Khorasan.
Syria	Syria operated under a federalist system during its period of French rule . Its constituents were organized on primarily ethno-religious lines: there were separate states for Maronites, Alawites, Druze and Turks. The federal system was abolished after the Syrian independence in 1946.
Greece	Greece entered World War II on 28 October 1940, when the Italian army invaded from Albania. The Greek army dealt the first victory for the Allies by defeating the invasion and pushing Mussolini"s forces back into Albania. Hitler was reluctantly forced to send his own forces to overcome Greece in April 1941, and delay the invasion of the Soviet Union by six weeks.

Chapter 5. The World of Rome

Chapter 5. The World of Rome

History
- History of the East Coast of the United States
- History of the Southern United States
- History of the United States
- List of National Historic Landmarks in North Carolina
- National Register of Historic Places listings in North Carolina

Regions

Larger cities

Smaller cities

Major Towns

Counties

Tetrarchy

The term Tetrarchy describes any system of government where power is divided among four individuals, but usually refers to the Tetrarchy instituted by Roman Emperor Diocletian in 293 CE, marking the end of the Crisis of the Third Century and the recovery of the Roman Empire. This Tetrarchy lasted until c.313 CE, when internecine conflict eliminated most of the claimants to power, leaving Constantine in the West and Licinius in the East.

The first phase, sometimes referred to as the Diarchy, involved the designation of the general Maximian as co-emperor - firstly as Caesar (junior emperor) in 285, followed by his promotion to Augustus in 286.

Western world

The Western world is a term that can have multiple meanings depending on its context. Accordingly, the basic definition of what constitutes "the West" varies, expanding and contracting over time, in relation to various historical circumstances. Some historians believe the West originated in the northern and eastern Mediterranean with ancient Greece and ancient Rome.

Byzantium

Byzantium was an ancient Greek city, which was founded by Greek colonists from Megara in 667 BC and named after their king Byzas or Byzantas. The name "Byzantium" is a Latinization of the original name Byzantion. The city is what later evolved to be the center of the Byzantine Empire under the name of Constantinople.

Chapter 5. The World of Rome

Chapter 6. East Asia and the Spread of Buddhism, 256 B.C.E.-800 C.E.

Qin Dynasty

The Qin Dynasty was the ruling Chinese dynasty between 221 and 206 BC. The Qin state was so named because its rulers were descendants of the first emperor"s ancestors whose fief was called "Qin". The Qin"s strength had been consolidated by Lord Shang Yang during the Warring States Period, in the 4th century BC. In the early third century BC, the Qin accomplished a series of swift conquests; the state subjugated the Chu, remnants of the Zhou Dynasty, and various other states to gain undisputed control of China.

During its reign over China, the Qin Dynasty enjoyed increased trade, agriculture, and military security.

Xianyang

Xianyang is a city in Shaanxi province, near Xi"an. The city site was located a few kilometers to the northwest of present-day Xi"an. It has an area of 10,213 square kilometers and a population of 4,800,000.

India

India, officially the Indian Empire, declared war on Germany in September 1939. The Provinces of India " href="/wiki/East_African_Campaign_(World_War_II)">East African Campaign, Western Desert Campaign and the Italian Campaign. At the height of the World War, more than 2.5 million Indian troops were fighting Axis forces around the globe.

Parthia

Parthia is a region of north-eastern Iran, best known for having been the political and cultural base of the Arsacid dynasts, after which the Arsacid Empire is then also known as the "Parthian Empire".

The name "Parthia" is a continuation from Latin Parthia, from Old Persian Parthava, which was the Parthian language self-designator signifying "of the Parthians".

Parthia roughly corresponds to the western half of Khorasan.

Empire

The term Empire derives from the Latin imperium. Politically, an Empire is a geographically extensive group of states and peoples united and ruled either by a monarch (emperor, empress) or an oligarchy. Geopolitically, the term Empire has denoted very different, territorially-extreme states -- at the strong end, the extensive Spanish Empire and the British Empire (19th c.), at the weak end, the Holy Roman Empire (8th c.-19th c.), in its Medieval and early-modern forms, and the Byzantine Empire (15th c.), that was a direct continuation of the Roman Empire, that, in its final century of existence, was more a city-state than a territorial Empire.

Imperialism

The term Imperialism commonly refers to a political or geographical domain such as the Ottoman Empire, the French Empire the Russian Empire, the Chinese Empire etc., but the term can equally be applied to domains of knowledge, beliefs, values and expertise, such as the empires of Christianity or Islam . Imperialism is usually autocratic, and also sometimes monolithic in character.

Imperialism is found in the ancient histories of the Assyrian Empire, Chinese Empire, Roman Empire, Greece, the Persian Empire, and the Ottoman Empire , ancient Egypt, India, the Aztec empire, and a basic component to the conquests of Genghis Khan and other warlords.

Roman

A Roman or civil diocese was one of the administrative divisions of the later Roman Empire, starting with the Tetrarchy. It formed the intermediate level of government, grouping several provinces and being in turn subordinated to a praetorian prefecture.

The earliest use of "diocese" as an administrative unit was in the Greek-speaking East.

Chapter 6. East Asia and the Spread of Buddhism, 256B.c.E.-800c.E.

Chapter 6. East Asia and the Spread of Buddhism, 256B.c.E.-800c.E.

Rome	Rome is the capital of Italy and the country"s largest and most populous city, with over 2.7 million residents in a municipality of some 1,285.3 km² (496.3 sq mi), while the population of the urban area is estimated by Eurostat to be 3.46 million. The metropolitan area of Rome is estimated by OECD to have a population of 3.7 million. It is located in the central-western portion of the Italian Peninsula, on the Tiber river.
Peasant	A Peasant is an agricultural worker who subsists by working a small plot of ground. The term Peasant today is sometimes used in a pejorative sense for impoverished farmers. Peasants typically make up the majority of the agricultural labour force in a Pre-industrial society, dependent on the cultivation of their land: without stockpiles of provisions they thrive or starve according to the most recent harvest.
Slavery	Slavery (Romanian: robie) existed on the territory of present-day Romania from before the founding of the principalities of Wallachia and Moldavia in 13th-14th century, until it was abolished in stages during the 1840s and 1850s. Most of the slaves were of Roma (Gypsy) ethnicity. Particularly in Moldavia there were also slaves of Tatar ethnicity, probably prisoners captured from the wars with the Nogai and Crimean Tatars.
Kushan empire	The Kushan Empire (c. 1st-3rd centuries CE) was originally formed in the territories of ancient Bactria on either side of the middle course of the Oxus River or Amu Darya in what is now northern Afghanistan, and southern Tajikistan and Uzbekistan. During the 1st and early 2nd centuries CE the Kushans expanded rapidly across the northern part of the Indian subcontinent at least as far as Sarnath near Varanasi (Benares) where inscriptions have been found dated to the first few years of era of the most famous Kushan ruler, Kanishka which apparently began about 127 CE. The Chinese history, the Hou Hanshu, gives an account of the formation of the Kushan Empire based on a report made by the Chinese general Ban Yong to the Chinese Emperor c.
Northern Wei	The Northern Wei Dynasty Later Wei was "part of an era of political turbulence and intense social and cultural change". It is perhaps most noted for the unification of northern China in 439, but was also a period when foreign ideas were introduced, and Buddhism became firmly established. Many antiques and art works, both Daoist and Buddhist, from this period have survived.
Capital	

Flag

The three occupation zones. Blue indicates the Italian, red the German and green the Bulgarian zones. The Italian zone was taken over by the Germans in September 1943.

Capital	Athens
Political structure	Puppet state
Prime Minister	
- 1941-1942	Georgios Tsolakoglou
- 1942-1943	Konst.

Chapter 6. East Asia and the Spread of Buddhism, 256B.c.E.-800c.E.

Chapter 6. East Asia and the Spread of Buddhism, 256B.c.E.-800c.E.

Sui Dynasty	The Sui Dynasty followed by the Tang Dynasty and preceded by the Southern and Northern Dynasties in China. It ended nearly four centuries of division between rival regimes. The Sui Dynasty founded by Emperor Wen, or Yang Jian, held its capital at Chang"an , also known during Sui as Daxing (å¤§è˜.)
Tang Dynasty	The Tang Dynasty was an imperial dynasty of China preceded by the Sui Dynasty and followed by the Five Dynasties and Ten Kingdoms Period. It was founded by the Li (æŽ) family, who seized power during the decline and collapse of the Sui Empire. The dynasty was interrupted briefly by the Second Zhou Dynasty (October 16, 690 - March 3, 705) when Empress Wu Zetian seized the throne, becoming the first and only Chinese empress regnant, ruling in her own right.
Ethnicity	Ethnicity plays a prominent role in pornography. Distinct genres of pornography focus on performers of specific ethnic groups, or on the depiction of interracial sexual activity. Ethnic pornography typically employs ethnic and racial stereotypes in its depiction of performers.
Silla	Silla (57 BC - 935 AD) (Korean pronunciation: [Éˆilla]) was one of the Three Kingdoms of Korea, and the longest sustained dynasty in Asian history. Although it was founded by King Park Hyeokgeose, who is also known to be the originator of the Korean family name Park (ë°•, æœ´), the dynasty was to see the Kyungju Kim (ê¹€, é‡‘) clan hold rule for most of its 992-year history. What began as a chiefdom in the Samhan confederacies, once allied with China, Silla eventually conquered the other two kingdoms, Baekje in 660 and Goguryeo in 668.
Japan	Japan participated in World War I from 1914 to 1917, as one of the major Entente Powers and played an important role in securing the sea lanes in South Pacific and Indian Oceans against the Kaiserliche Marine. Politically, Japan seized the opportunity to expand its sphere of influence in China, and to gain recognition as a great power in postwar geopolitics. On 7 August 1914, the Japanese government received an official request from the British government for assistance in destroying the German raiders of the Kaiserliche Marine in and around Chinese waters.

Chapter 7. The Making of Europe

Empire The term Empire derives from the Latin imperium. Politically, an Empire is a geographically extensive group of states and peoples united and ruled either by a monarch (emperor, empress) or an oligarchy. Geopolitically, the term Empire has denoted very different, territorially-extreme states -- at the strong end, the extensive Spanish Empire and the British Empire (19th c)., at the weak end, the Holy Roman Empire (8th c.-19th c.), in its Medieval and early-modern forms, and the Byzantine Empire (15th c.), that was a direct continuation of the Roman Empire, that, in its final century of existence, was more a city-state than a territorial Empire.

Roman A Roman or civil diocese was one of the administrative divisions of the later Roman Empire, starting with the Tetrarchy. It formed the intermediate level of government, grouping several provinces and being in turn subordinated to a praetorian prefecture.
The earliest use of "diocese" as an administrative unit was in the Greek-speaking East.

Rome Rome is the capital of Italy and the country"s largest and most populous city, with over 2.7 million residents in a municipality of some 1,285.3 km^2 (496.3 sq mi), while the population of the urban area is estimated by Eurostat to be 3.46 million. The metropolitan area of Rome is estimated by OECD to have a population of 3.7 million. It is located in the central-western portion of the Italian Peninsula, on the Tiber river.

Law The great end, for which men entered into society, was to secure their property. That right is preserved sacred and incommunicable in all instances, where it has not been taken away or abridged by some public Law for the good of the whole ... If no excuse can be found or produced, the silence of the books is an authority against the defendant, and the plaintiff must have judgment.

Italy Italy (Italian: Italia), officially the Italian Republic (Italian: Repubblica Italiana), is a country located on the Italian Peninsula in Southern Europe and on the two largest islands in the Mediterranean Sea, Sicily and Sardinia. Italy shares its northern, Alpine boundary with France, Switzerland, Austria and Slovenia. The independent states of San Marino and the Vatican City are enclaves within the Italian Peninsula, and Campione d"Italia is an Italian exclave in Switzerland.

Roman Empire The Roman Empire was the post-Republican phase of the ancient Roman civilization, characterised by an autocratic form of government and large territorial holdings in Europe and around the Mediterranean. The term is used to describe the Roman state during and after the time of the first emperor, Augustus. The nearly 500-year-old Roman Republic, which preceded it, had been weakened by several civil wars.

Western Roman Empire The Western Roman Empire refers to the western half of the Roman Empire, from its division by Diocletian in 285; the other half of the Roman Empire was the Eastern Roman Empire, today widely known as the Byzantine Empire.
The Western Empire existed intermittently in several periods between the 3rd century and 5th century, after Diocletian"s Tetrarchy and the reunifications associated with Constantine the Great and Julian the Apostate (324-363.) Theodosius I (379-395) was the last Roman Emperor who ruled over a unified Roman empire.

Day A Day (symbol d) is a unit of time equivalent to approximately 24 hours. It is not an SI unit but it is accepted for use with SI. The SI unit of time is the second.

Chapter 7. The Making of Europe

Chapter 7. The Making of Europe

	The word "Day" can also refer to the (roughly) half of the Day that is not night, also known as "Daytime".
Alexandria	Alexandria located in the Iranian land of harauti known by the Greeks as Arachosia, was one of the seventy-plus cities founded or renamed by Alexander the Great. It is believed to be in proximity of modern day Quetta Pakistan. Arachosia is the Greek name of an ancient province of the Achaemenid, Seleucid and Parthian empires.
India	India, officially the Indian Empire, declared war on Germany in September 1939. The Provinces of India " href="/wiki/East_African_Campaign_(World_War_II)">East African Campaign, Western Desert Campaign and the Italian Campaign. At the height of the World War, more than 2.5 million Indian troops were fighting Axis forces around the globe.
Ethnicity	Ethnicity plays a prominent role in pornography. Distinct genres of pornography focus on performers of specific ethnic groups, or on the depiction of interracial sexual activity. Ethnic pornography typically employs ethnic and racial stereotypes in its depiction of performers.
Romanization	In linguistics, Romanization or latinization, alternately spelt as latinisation or romanisation , is the representation of a written word or spoken speech with the Roman alphabet where the original word or language uses a different writing system (or none). Methods of Romanization include transliteration, for representing written text, and transcription, for representing the spoken word. The latter can be subdivided into phonemic transcription, which records the phonemes or units of semantic meaning in speech, and more strict phonetic transcription, which records speech sounds with precision.
Greece	Greece entered World War II on 28 October 1940, when the Italian army invaded from Albania. The Greek army dealt the first victory for the Allies by defeating the invasion and pushing Mussolini"s forces back into Albania. Hitler was reluctantly forced to send his own forces to overcome Greece in April 1941, and delay the invasion of the Soviet Union by six weeks.
Ottoman	The state of the Ottomans which began as part of the Anatolian Seljuk Sultanate and became an independent Empire, has been known historically by different names at different periods and in various languages. This page surveys the history of these names and their usage. · Modern Turkish: OsmanlÄ± BeyliÄŸi; The first declaration of statehood happened under Osman I. · Ä€l-e UṩmÄ n

Chapter 7. The Making of Europe

Chapter 7. The Making of Europe

- Medieval Latin: Turchia
- Medieval Latin: Imperium Turcicum
- English: Turkey ; the current use of the name Turkey refers to the Republic of Turkey which succeeded the Ottoman Empire in 1923
- English: Turkish Empire, Ottoman Empire, Osmanic Empire, Osmanian Empire
- Ottoman Turkish/Persian: دولت علیه عثمانیه Devlet-i Âliye-yi Osmâniyye
- Ottoman Turkish/Persian: Devlet-i Âliye (The Sublime State)
- Ottoman Turkish/Persian: Devlet-i Ebed-Müddet
- Ottoman Turkish/Persian: Memâlik-i Mahrûse (The Well-Protected Domains)
- Ottoman Turkish/Persian: Memâlik-i Mahrûse-i Osmanî
- Modern Turkish: Osmanlı İmparatorluğu (Ottoman Empire),
- Arabic: الدولة العلية العثمانية Ad-Dawlat al-ʿAlīyah al-ʿUthmānīyah
- Bulgarian: Османска империя (Osmanska Imperia)
- Greek: Οθωμανική Αυτοκρατορία
- Armenian: Օսմանյան Կայսրություն (Osmanyan Kaysroutyoun)

In diplomatic circles, the Ottoman government was often referred to as the "Sublime Porte", a literal translation of the Ottoman Turkish Bâb-ı Âlî, which was the only gate of the imperial Topkapı Palace that was open to foreigners, and where the Sultan, Grand Vizier or Viziers greeted the ambassadors.

Ottoman Turks — The Ottoman Turks were the subdivision of the Ottoman Muslim Millet that dominated the ruling class of the Ottoman Empire. Reliable information about the early history of the Ottomans is scarce. According to some sources (references needed), the leader (khan) of the Kayi tribe of the Oguz Turks, Ertugrul, left Persia in the mid-thirteenth century to escape the invading Mongols.

Parthia — Parthia is a region of north-eastern Iran, best known for having been the political and cultural base of the Arsacid dynasts, after which the Arsacid Empire is then also known as the "Parthian Empire".

The name "Parthia" is a continuation from Latin Parthia, from Old Persian Parthava, which was the Parthian language self-designator signifying "of the Parthians".

Parthia roughly corresponds to the western half of Khorasan.

Chalcedon — Chalcedon was an ancient maritime town of Bithynia, in Asia Minor, almost directly opposite Byzantium, south of Scutari . Today, in modern Turkish, Chalcedon is called Kadıköy, and is a district of Istanbul, Turkey. The variant Calchedon is found on all the coins of Chalcedon as well as in manuscripts of Herodotus"s Histories, Xenophon"s Hellenica, Arrian"s Anabasis and other works.

Western world — The Western world is a term that can have multiple meanings depending on its context . Accordingly, the basic definition of what constitutes "the West" varies, expanding and contracting over time, in relation to various historical circumstances. Some historians believe the West originated in the northern and eastern Mediterranean with ancient Greece and ancient Rome.

Chapter 7. The Making of Europe

Chapter 7. The Making of Europe

History	· History of the East Coast of the United States · History of the Southern United States · History of the United States · List of National Historic Landmarks in North Carolina · National Register of Historic Places listings in North Carolina
Regions	
Larger cities	
Smaller cities	
Major Towns	
Counties	
Alexander	Alexander was tagus or despot of Pherae in Thessaly, and ruled from 369 BC to 358 BC. The accounts of his usurpation vary somewhat in minor points. Diodorus Siculus tells us that on the assassination of his father, the tyrant Jason of Pherae, in 370 BC, his brother Polydorus ruled for a year, and was then poisoned by Alexander, another brother. According to Xenophon, Polydorus was murdered by his brother Polyphron, and Polyphron, in 369 BC murdered by Alexander--his nephew, according to Plutarch, who relates also that Alexander worshiped the spear with which he slew his uncle as if it was a god.
Aristocracy	Aristocracy is a form of government, in which a select few such as the most wise, strong or contributing citizens rule, often starting as a system of co-option where a council of prominent citizens add leading soldiers, merchants, land owners, priests, or lawyers to their number. Aristocracy deforms when it becomes hereditary elite. Aristocracies have most often been deformed to hereditary plutocratic systems.

Chapter 7. The Making of Europe

Chapter 8. The Islamic World, ca 600-1400

Empire	The term Empire derives from the Latin imperium. Politically, an Empire is a geographically extensive group of states and peoples united and ruled either by a monarch (emperor, empress) or an oligarchy. Geopolitically, the term Empire has denoted very different, territorially-extreme states -- at the strong end, the extensive Spanish Empire and the British Empire (19th c.), at the weak end, the Holy Roman Empire (8th c.-19th c.), in its Medieval and early-modern forms, and the Byzantine Empire (15th c.), that was a direct continuation of the Roman Empire, that, in its final century of existence, was more a city-state than a territorial Empire.
Umma	Umma (modern Tell Jokha) was an ancient city in Sumer. Best known for its long frontier conflict with Lagash. The city reached its zenith ca.
Law	The great end, for which men entered into society, was to secure their property. That right is preserved sacred and incommunicable in all instances, where it has not been taken away or abridged by some public Law for the good of the whole ... If no excuse can be found or produced, the silence of the books is an authority against the defendant, and the plaintiff must have judgment.
Alexandria	Alexandria located in the Iranian land of harauti known by the Greeks as Arachosia, was one of the seventy-plus cities founded or renamed by Alexander the Great. It is believed to be in proximity of modern day Quetta Pakistan. Arachosia is the Greek name of an ancient province of the Achaemenid, Seleucid and Parthian empires.
Athens	Athens , the capital and largest city of Greece, dominates the Attica periphery; as one of the world"s oldest cities, its recorded history spans around 3,400 years. The Greek capital has a population of 745,514 within its administrative limits and a land area of 39 km^2 (15 sq mi). The urban area of Athens extends beyond the administrative city limits with a population of 3,130,841 (in 2001) and a land area of 412 km^2 (159 sq mi).
Roman	A Roman or civil diocese was one of the administrative divisions of the later Roman Empire, starting with the Tetrarchy. It formed the intermediate level of government, grouping several provinces and being in turn subordinated to a praetorian prefecture. The earliest use of "diocese" as an administrative unit was in the Greek-speaking East.
Roman Empire	The Roman Empire was the post-Republican phase of the ancient Roman civilization, characterised by an autocratic form of government and large territorial holdings in Europe and around the Mediterranean. The term is used to describe the Roman state during and after the time of the first emperor, Augustus. The nearly 500-year-old Roman Republic, which preceded it, had been weakened by several civil wars.
Sparta	Sparta was an important Greek city-state in the Peloponnesus. It was unusual among Greek city-states in that it maintained its kingship past the Archaic age. It was even more unusual in that it had two kings simultaneously, coming from two separate lines.

Chapter 8. The Islamic World, ca 600-1400

Chapter 8. The Islamic World, ca 600-1400

Hebron	Hebron â€Ž al-á¸ªalÄ«l or al-KhalÄ«l; Hebrew: Â·)â€Ž, Hevron, Tiberian Hebrew: á¸¤eá¸‡rôn) is the largest city in the West Bank, located in the south, 30 kilometers south of Jerusalem. It is home to some 166,000 Palestinians, and over 500 Israelis. Hebron lies 930 meters above sea level.
Syria	Syria operated under a federalist system during its period of French rule . Its constituents were organized on primarily ethno-religious lines: there were separate states for Maronites, Alawites, Druze and Turks. The federal system was abolished after the Syrian independence in 1946.
Slavery	Slavery (Romanian: robie) existed on the territory of present-day Romania from before the founding of the principalities of Wallachia and Moldavia in 13th-14th century, until it was abolished in stages during the 1840s and 1850s. Most of the slaves were of Roma (Gypsy) ethnicity. Particularly in Moldavia there were also slaves of Tatar ethnicity, probably prisoners captured from the wars with the Nogai and Crimean Tatars.
Rome	Rome is the capital of Italy and the country"s largest and most populous city, with over 2.7 million residents in a municipality of some 1,285.3 km^2 (496.3 sq mi), while the population of the urban area is estimated by Eurostat to be 3.46 million. The metropolitan area of Rome is estimated by OECD to have a population of 3.7 million. It is located in the central-western portion of the Italian Peninsula, on the Tiber river.
Factory	A Factory (previously manuFactory) or manufacturing plant is an industrial building where workers manufacture goods or supervise machines processing one product into another. Most modern factories have large warehouses or warehouse-like facilities that contain heavy equipment used for assembly line production. Typically, factories gather and concentrate resources: workers, capital and plant.
India	India, officially the Indian Empire, declared war on Germany in September 1939. The Provinces of India " href="/wiki/East_African_Campaign_(World_War_II)">East African Campaign, Western Desert Campaign and the Italian Campaign. At the height of the World War, more than 2.5 million Indian troops were fighting Axis forces around the globe.
Philippines	The Philippines (Tagalog: Pilipinas [pÉªlÉªËˆpinÉ s]) officially known as the Republic of the Philippines, is a country in Southeast Asia with Manila as its capital city. It comprises 7,107 islands in the western Pacific Ocean. The Philippines is the world"s 12th most populous country, with an estimated population of about 92 million people.
Parthia	Parthia is a region of north-eastern Iran, best known for having been the political and cultural base of the Arsacid dynasts, after which the Arsacid Empire is then also known as the "Parthian Empire". The name "Parthia" is a continuation from Latin Parthia, from Old Persian Parthava, which was the Parthian language self-designator signifying "of the Parthians". Parthia roughly corresponds to the western half of Khorasan.

Chapter 8. The Islamic World, ca 600-1400

Chapter 8. The Islamic World, ca 600-1400

History	· History of the East Coast of the United States · History of the Southern United States · History of the United States · List of National Historic Landmarks in North Carolina · National Register of Historic Places listings in North Carolina
Regions	
Larger cities	
Smaller cities	
Major Towns	
Counties	
Politics	Politics is a process by which groups of people make decisions. The term is generally applied to behavior within civil governments, but Politics has been observed in all human group interactions, including corporate, academic and religious institutions. It consists of "social relations involving authority or power" and refers to the regulation of a political unit, and to the methods and tactics used to formulate and apply policy.
Republic	A Republic is a form of government in which the head of state is not a monarch and the people (or at least a part of its people) have an impact on its government. The word "Republic" is derived from the Latin phrase res publica which can be translated as "public affairs". Both modern and ancient Republics vary widely in their ideology and composition.
Capital	

Flag

The three occupation zones. Blue indicates the Italian, red the German and green the Bulgarian zones. The Italian zone was taken over by the Germans in September 1943.

Capital   Athens
Political structure   Puppet state
Prime Minister
- 1941-1942   Georgios Tsolakoglou
- 1942-1943   Konst.

Chapter 8. The Islamic World, ca 600-1400

Chapter 9. African Societies and Kingdoms, ca 400-1450

Empire

The term Empire derives from the Latin imperium. Politically, an Empire is a geographically extensive group of states and peoples united and ruled either by a monarch (emperor, empress) or an oligarchy. Geopolitically, the term Empire has denoted very different, territorially-extreme states -- at the strong end, the extensive Spanish Empire and the British Empire (19th c.), at the weak end, the Holy Roman Empire (8th c.-19th c.), in its Medieval and early-modern forms, and the Byzantine Empire (15th c.), that was a direct continuation of the Roman Empire, that, in its final century of existence, was more a city-state than a territorial Empire.

Ottoman

The state of the Ottomans which began as part of the Anatolian Seljuk Sultanate and became an independent Empire, has been known historically by different names at different periods and in various languages. This page surveys the history of these names and their usage.

· Modern Turkish: OsmanlÄ± BeyliÄŸi;
The first declaration of statehood happened under Osman I.

· Ä€l-e Uá'mÄ n

· Medieval Latin: Turchia
· Medieval Latin: Imperium Turcicum
· English: Turkey ; the current use of the name Turkey refers to the Republic of Turkey which succeeded the Ottoman Empire in 1923
· English: Turkish Empire, Ottoman Empire, Osmanic Empire, Osmanian Empire
· Ottoman Turkish/Persian: Ø¯ÙˆÙ„Øª Ø¹Ù„ÙŠÙ‡ Ø¹Ø«Ù…Ø§Ù†ÙŠÙ‡ Devlet-i Âliye-yi Osmâniyye
· Ottoman Turkish/Persian: Devlet-i Âliye (The Sublime State)
· Ottoman Turkish/Persian: Devlet-i Ebed-Müddet
· Ottoman Turkish/Persian: Memâlik-i Mahrûse (The Well-Protected Domains)
· Ottoman Turkish/Persian: Memâlik-i Mahrûse-i Osmanî
· Modern Turkish: OsmanlÄ± Ä°mparatorluÄŸu (Ottoman Empire),
· Arabic: Ø§Ù„Ø¯ÙˆÙ„Ø© Ø§Ù„Ø¹Ù„ÙŠØ© Ø§Ù„Ø¹Ø«Ù…Ø§Ù†ÙŠØ© Ad-Dawlat al-ʻĀlīa al-ʻUthmā nīa
· Bulgarian: Ožн Ð¼Ð°Ð½Ñ Ð°Ð° Ð¸Ð¼Ð¿ÐµÑ€Ð¸Ñ (Osmanska Imperia)
· Greek: ΟθωμανικÎ® ΑυτοκρατορΓ α
· Armenian: Օ•Õ½Õ´Õ¡Õ¶Õ¶Õ¸Õ¡Õ¶ Օ¿Օ¡Õ½Õ¾Õ€Õ¸Ö•Õ©Õ¸Õ¶ (Osmanyan Kaysroutyoun)
In diplomatic circles, the Ottoman government was often referred to as the "Sublime Porte", a literal translation of the Ottoman Turkish Bâb-Ä± Âlî, which was the only gate of the imperial TopkapÄ± Palace that was open to foreigners, and where the Sultan, Grand Vizier or Viziers greeted the ambassadors.

Ottoman Empire

The Ottoman Empire or Ottoman State , also known by its contemporaries as the Turkish Empire or Turkey , was an empire that lasted from 1299 to November 1, 1922 (as an imperial monarchy) or July 24, 1923 (de jure, as a state.) It was succeeded by the Republic of Turkey, which was officially proclaimed on October 29, 1923.

At the height of its power (16th-17th century), it spanned three continents, controlling much of Southeastern Europe, Western Asia and North Africa.

Chapter 9. African Societies and Kingdoms, ca 400-1450

Chapter 9. African Societies and Kingdoms, ca 400-1450

Roman	A Roman or civil diocese was one of the administrative divisions of the later Roman Empire, starting with the Tetrarchy. It formed the intermediate level of government, grouping several provinces and being in turn subordinated to a praetorian prefecture. The earliest use of "diocese" as an administrative unit was in the Greek-speaking East.
Aristocracy	Aristocracy is a form of government, in which a select few such as the most wise, strong or contributing citizens rule, often starting as a system of co-option where a council of prominent citizens add leading soldiers, merchants, land owners, priests, or lawyers to their number. Aristocracy deforms when it becomes hereditary elite. Aristocracies have most often been deformed to hereditary plutocratic systems.
Nigeria	Nigeria , officially the Federal Republic of Nigeria, is a federal constitutional republic comprising thirty-six states and one Federal Capital Territory. The country is located in West Africa and shares land borders with the Republic of Benin in the west, Chad and Cameroon in the east, and Niger in the north. Its coast lies on the Gulf of Guinea, a part of the Atlantic Ocean, in the south.
Nazi Germany	Nazi Germany and the Third Reich are the common English names for Germany between 1933 and 1945, while it was led by Adolf Hitler and the National Socialist German Worker"s Party . The name Third Reich (Drittes Reich, "Third Reich") refers to the state as the successor to the Holy Roman Empire of the Middle Ages and the German Empire of 1871-1918. In German, the state was known as Deutsches Reich until 1943, when its official name became Großdeutsches Reich .
Slavery	Slavery (Romanian: robie) existed on the territory of present-day Romania from before the founding of the principalities of Wallachia and Moldavia in 13th-14th century, until it was abolished in stages during the 1840s and 1850s. Most of the slaves were of Roma (Gypsy) ethnicity. Particularly in Moldavia there were also slaves of Tatar ethnicity, probably prisoners captured from the wars with the Nogai and Crimean Tatars.
Mali	Mali, officially the Republic of Mali , is a landlocked nation in Western Africa. Mali is the seventh largest country in Africa, bordering Algeria on the north, Niger on the east, Burkina Faso and the Côte d"Ivoire on the south, Guinea on the south-west, and Senegal and Mauritania on the west. Its size is just over 1,240,000 km^2 with an estimated population of about 13,000,000. Its capital is Bamako.
Alexandria	Alexandria located in the Iranian land of harauti known by the Greeks as Arachosia, was one of the seventy-plus cities founded or renamed by Alexander the Great. It is believed to be in proximity of modern day Quetta Pakistan. Arachosia is the Greek name of an ancient province of the Achaemenid, Seleucid and Parthian empires.
India	India, officially the Indian Empire, declared war on Germany in September 1939. The Provinces of India " href="/wiki/East_African_Campaign_(World_War_II)">East African Campaign, Western Desert Campaign and the Italian Campaign. At the height of the World War, more than 2.5 million Indian troops were fighting Axis forces around the globe.
Ifat	Ifat was a Muslim sultanate covering eastern Shewa and located in modern day Ethiopia.

	The historian al-Umari, records that it was near the Red Sea coast, and states its size as 15 days travel by 20 days travel; its army numbered 15,000 horsemen and 20,000 foot. Al-Umar also credits it with seven "mother cities": Belquizar, Kuljura, Shimi, Shewa, Adal, Jamme, and Laboo.
Malindi	Malindi (once known as Melinde) is a town on Malindi Bay at the mouth of the Galana River, lying on the Indian Ocean coast of Kenya. It is 120 kilometres northeast of Mombasa. The population of Malindi is 117,735 (in 1999 census).
Mombasa	Mombasa is the second largest city in Kenya, lying on the Indian Ocean. It has a major port and an international airport. The city is the centre of the coastal tourism industry.
Zanzibar	Zanzibar is a semi-autonomous part of the United Republic of Tanzania, in East Africa. It comprises the Zanzibar Archipelago in the Indian Ocean, 25-50 kilometres off the coast of the mainland, and consists of numerous small islands and two large ones: Unguja (the main island, informally referred to as Zanzibar), and Pemba. Zanzibar was once a separate state with a long trading history within the Arab world; it united with Tanganyika to form Tanzania in 1964 and still enjoys a high degree of autonomy within the union. The capital of Zanzibar, located on the island of Unguja, is Zanzibar City, and its historic center, known as Stone Town, is a World Heritage Site.

Chapter 9. African Societies and Kingdoms, ca 400-1450

Chapter 10. Central and Southern Asia, to 1400

Empire

The term Empire derives from the Latin imperium. Politically, an Empire is a geographically extensive group of states and peoples united and ruled either by a monarch (emperor, empress) or an oligarchy. Geopolitically, the term Empire has denoted very different, territorially-extreme states -- at the strong end, the extensive Spanish Empire and the British Empire (19th c.), at the weak end, the Holy Roman Empire (8th c.-19th c.), in its Medieval and early-modern forms, and the Byzantine Empire (15th c.), that was a direct continuation of the Roman Empire, that, in its final century of existence, was more a city-state than a territorial Empire.

Mongolia

Mongolia , literally Mongol country/nation,) is a landlocked country in East and Central Asia. It borders Russia to the north and the People"s Republic of China to the south, east and west. Although Mongolia does not share a border with Kazakhstan, its western-most point is only 24 miles from Kazakhstan"s eastern tip.

Ottoman

The state of the Ottomans which began as part of the Anatolian Seljuk Sultanate and became an independent Empire, has been known historically by different names at different periods and in various languages. This page surveys the history of these names and their usage.

· Modern Turkish: OsmanlÄ± BeyliÄŸi;
The first declaration of statehood happened under Osman I.

· Ä€l-e Uá'mÄ n

· Medieval Latin: Turchia
· Medieval Latin: Imperium Turcicum
· English: Turkey ; the current use of the name Turkey refers to the Republic of Turkey which succeeded the Ottoman Empire in 1923
· English: Turkish Empire, Ottoman Empire, Osmanic Empire, Osmanian Empire
· Ottoman Turkish/Persian: Ø¯ÙˆÙ„Øª Ø¹Ù„ÙŠÙ‡ Ø¹Ø«Ù…Ø§Ù†ÙŠÙ‡ Devlet-i Âliye-yi Osmâniyye
· Ottoman Turkish/Persian: Devlet-i Âliye (The Sublime State)
· Ottoman Turkish/Persian: Devlet-i Ebed-Müddet
· Ottoman Turkish/Persian: Memâlik-i Mahrûse (The Well-Protected Domains)
· Ottoman Turkish/Persian: Memâlik-i Mahrûse-i Osmanî
· Modern Turkish: OsmanlÄ± Ä°mparatorluÄŸu (Ottoman Empire),
· Arabic: Ø§Ù„Ø¯ÙˆÙ„Ø© Ø§Ù„Ø¹Ù„ÙŠØ© Ø§Ù„Ø¹Ù…...Ø§Ù†ÙŠØ© Ad-Dawlat al-Ë¤Ä€lÄ« al-Ë¤UthmÄ nÄ«
· Bulgarian: ÐžÑ Ð¼Ð°Ð½Ñ ÐºÐ° Ð˜Ð¼Ð¿ÐµÑ€Ð¸Ñ (Osmanska Imperia)
· Greek: ΟθωμανικÎ® ΑυτοκρατορÎ―α
· Armenian: Օսմանյան Կայսրություն (Osmanyan Kaysroutyoun)
In diplomatic circles, the Ottoman government was often referred to as the "Sublime Porte", a literal translation of the Ottoman Turkish Bâb-Ä± Âlî, which was the only gate of the imperial TopkapÄ± Palace that was open to foreigners, and where the Sultan, Grand Vizier or Viziers greeted the ambassadors.

Chapter 10. Central and Southern Asia, to 1400

Chapter 10. Central and Southern Asia, to 1400

Ottoman Empire	The Ottoman Empire or Ottoman State, also known by its contemporaries as the Turkish Empire or Turkey, was an empire that lasted from 1299 to November 1, 1922 (as an imperial monarchy) or July 24, 1923 (de jure, as a state.) It was succeeded by the Republic of Turkey, which was officially proclaimed on October 29, 1923. At the height of its power (16th-17th century), it spanned three continents, controlling much of Southeastern Europe, Western Asia and North Africa.
Ottoman Turks	The Ottoman Turks were the subdivision of the Ottoman Muslim Millet that dominated the ruling class of the Ottoman Empire. Reliable information about the early history of the Ottomans is scarce. According to some sources (references needed), the leader (khan) of the Kayi tribe of the Oguz Turks, Ertugrul, left Persia in the mid-thirteenth century to escape the invading Mongols.
Ghaznavid	The Ghaznavids were an Islamic and Persianate dynasty of Turkic mamluk origin which existed from 975 to 1187 and ruled much of Persia, Transoxania, and the northern parts of the Indian subcontinent. The Ghaznavid state was centered in Ghazni, a city in present Afghanistan. Due to the political and cultural influence of their predecessors - that of the Persian Samanid Empire - the originally Turkic Ghaznavids became thoroughly Persianized.
Rome	Rome is the capital of Italy and the country"s largest and most populous city, with over 2.7 million residents in a municipality of some 1,285.3 km^2 (496.3 sq mi), while the population of the urban area is estimated by Eurostat to be 3.46 million. The metropolitan area of Rome is estimated by OECD to have a population of 3.7 million. It is located in the central-western portion of the Italian Peninsula, on the Tiber river.
Roman	A Roman or civil diocese was one of the administrative divisions of the later Roman Empire, starting with the Tetrarchy. It formed the intermediate level of government, grouping several provinces and being in turn subordinated to a praetorian prefecture. The earliest use of "diocese" as an administrative unit was in the Greek-speaking East.
History	· History of the East Coast of the United States · History of the Southern United States · History of the United States · List of National Historic Landmarks in North Carolina · National Register of Historic Places listings in North Carolina
Regions	
Larger cities	
Smaller cities	
Major Towns	
Counties	

Chapter 10. Central and Southern Asia, to 1400

Chapter 10. Central and Southern Asia, to 1400

Karakorum — Karakorum (Khalkha Mongolian: Kharkhorin, Classical Mongolian: Qara Qorum) was the capital of the Mongol Empire in the 13th century, although for only about 30 years. Its ruins lie in the northwestern corner of the Övörkhangai Province of Mongolia, near today"s town of Kharkhorin, and adjacent to the Erdene Zuu monastery. They are part of the upper part of the World Heritage Site Orkhon Valley Cultural Landscape.

Kamikaze — The Kamikaze) were suicide attacks by military aviators from the Empire of Japan against Allied naval vessels in the closing stages of the Pacific campaign of World War II, designed to destroy as many warships as possible.
Kamikaze pilots would attempt to intentionally crash their aircraft - often laden with explosives, bombs, torpedoes and full fuel tanks - into Allied ships. The aircraft"s normal functions, to deliver torpedoes or bombs or shoot down other aircraft, were put aside, and the planes were converted to what were essentially manned missiles, in a desperate attempt to reap the benefits of greatly increased accuracy and payload over that of normal bombs.

Nanzhao — Nanzhao, alternate spellings Nanchao and Nan Chao was a polity that flourished in what is now southern China and Southeast Asia during the 8th and 9th centuries. It was centered around present-day Yunnan in China. Asia in 800AD, showing Nanzhao and its neighbors.
Originally, there were several tribes that settled on the fertile land around Erhai lake.

Ethnicity — Ethnicity plays a prominent role in pornography. Distinct genres of pornography focus on performers of specific ethnic groups, or on the depiction of interracial sexual activity. Ethnic pornography typically employs ethnic and racial stereotypes in its depiction of performers.

Golden Horde — The Ulus of Jochi or the Golden Horde is an East Slavic designation for the Mongol--later Turkicized--Muslim khanate established in the western part of the Mongol Empire after the Mongol invasion of Rus" in the 1240s: present-day Russia, Ukraine, Moldova, Kazakhstan, and the Caucasus. Also known as Jochi ulus or Kipchak Khanate (not to be confused with the earlier Kipchak khanate prior to its conquest by the Mongols), the territory of the Golden Horde at its peak included most of Eastern Europe from the Urals to the right banks of the Dnieper River, extending east deep into Siberia. On the south, the Golden Horde"s lands bordered on the Black Sea, the Caucasus Mountains, and the territories of the Mongol dynasty known as the Ilkhanate.

Khaidu — According to the Secret History of the Mongols, a blue wolf and his mate, a fallow deer, settled at the head of the Onon River, and there, Batchilaguun (Batacaciqian), the ancestor of the Mongols, was born. Many generations passed and different clans emerged from the line of Batacaciqian. In the Borjigin clan there was a man named Khaidu.

Gupta Empire — The Gupta Empire (Hindi: à¤—à¥ à¤ªà¥ à¤¤ à¤°à¤¾à¤œà¤µà¤‚à¤¶ Gupta RÄ javaá¹fÅ›a) was an Ancient Indian empire which existed approximately from 280 to 550 AD and covered much of the Indian Subcontinent. Founded by Maharaja Sri-Gupta, the dynasty began the Classical Age in the Middle kingdoms of India. The capital of the Guptas was Pataliputra, present day Patna, in the north Indian state of Bihar.

India	India, officially the Indian Empire, declared war on Germany in September 1939. The Provinces of India " href="/wiki/East_African_Campaign_(World_War_II)">East African Campaign, Western Desert Campaign and the Italian Campaign. At the height of the World War, more than 2.5 million Indian troops were fighting Axis forces around the globe.
Mali	Mali, officially the Republic of Mali, is a landlocked nation in Western Africa. Mali is the seventh largest country in Africa, bordering Algeria on the north, Niger on the east, Burkina Faso and the Côte d"Ivoire on the south, Guinea on the south-west, and Senegal and Mauritania on the west. Its size is just over 1,240,000 km² with an estimated population of about 13,000,000. Its capital is Bamako.
Nigeria	Nigeria, officially the Federal Republic of Nigeria, is a federal constitutional republic comprising thirty-six states and one Federal Capital Territory. The country is located in West Africa and shares land borders with the Republic of Benin in the west, Chad and Cameroon in the east, and Niger in the north. Its coast lies on the Gulf of Guinea, a part of the Atlantic Ocean, in the south.
Vassal states	Vassal States were a number of tributary or Vassal States, usually on the periphery of the Ottoman Empire under suzerainty of the Porte, over which direct control was not established, for various reasons. Some of these states served as buffer states between the Ottomans and Christendom in Europe or Shi"ism in Asia. Their number varied over time but notable were the Khanate of Crimea, Wallachia, Moldavia, Transylvania, and the Kurdish Emirates.
Delhi sultanate	The Delhi Sultanate refers to the many Muslim states that ruled in India from 1206 to 1526. Several Turkic and Afghan dynasties ruled from Delhi: the Mamluk dynasty (1206-90), the Khilji dynasty (1290-1320), the Tughlaq dynasty (1320-1413), the Sayyid dynasty (1414-51), and the Lodhi dynasty (1451-1526). In 1526 the Delhi Sultanate was absorbed by the emerging Mughal Empire.
Law	The great end, for which men entered into society, was to secure their property. That right is preserved sacred and incommunicable in all instances, where it has not been taken away or abridged by some public Law for the good of the whole ... If no excuse can be found or produced, the silence of the books is an authority against the defendant, and the plaintiff must have judgment.
Funan	Funan was an ancient pre-Angkor Indianized kingdom located around the Mekong Delta. The ethno-linguistic nature of the people ; wether they were mostly Mon-Khmer or Austronesian, is the subject of much discussion among specialists. It is believed to have been established in the first century C.E. in the Mekong delta, which today is Vietnamese territory, although extensive human settlement in the region may have gone back as far as the 4th century B.C.E. Though regarded by Chinese envoys as a single unified empire, Funan may have been a collection of city-states that sometimes warred with one another and at other times constituted a political unity.

Chapter 10. Central and Southern Asia, to 1400

Chapter 10. Central and Southern Asia, to 1400

Tang Dynasty	The Tang Dynasty was an imperial dynasty of China preceded by the Sui Dynasty and followed by the Five Dynasties and Ten Kingdoms Period. It was founded by the Li (æ Ž) family, who seized power during the decline and collapse of the Sui Empire. The dynasty was interrupted briefly by the Second Zhou Dynasty (October 16, 690 - March 3, 705) when Empress Wu Zetian seized the throne, becoming the first and only Chinese empress regnant, ruling in her own right.
Peru-Bolivian Confederation	The Peru-Bolivian Confederation (or Confederacy) was a short-lived confederated state that existed in South America between the years 1836 and 1839. Its first and only head of state, titled Supreme Protector, was the Bolivian president, Marshal Andrés de Santa Cruz. The Confederation was a loose union between the states of Peru (by this time divided into a Republic of North Peru and a Republic of South Peru, which included the capital Tacna) and Bolivia.
Inca Empire	The Inca Empire (or Inka Empire) was the largest empire in pre-Columbian America. The administrative, political and military center of the empire was located in Cusco in modern-day Peru. The Inca Empire arose from the highlands of Peru sometime in early 13th century. From 1438 to 1533, the Incas used a variety of methods, from conquest to peaceful assimilation, to incorporate a large portion of western South America, centered on the Andean mountain ranges, including large parts of modern Ecuador, Peru, western and south central Bolivia, northwest Argentina, north and north-central Chile, and southern Colombia.
Khmer Empire	The Khmer Empire was the third largest empire of South East Asia (after Srivijaya and Majapahit), based in what is now Cambodia. The empire, which seceded from the kingdom of Chenla, at times ruled over and/or vassalised parts of modern-day Laos, Thailand, Vietnam, Myanmar, and Malaysia. During the formation of the empire, Khmer had close cultural, political and trade relations with Java, and later with Srivijaya empire that lay beyond Khmer"s southern border.
Srivijaya	Srivijaya or Sriwijaya was an ancient Malay kingdom on the island of Sumatra, Southeast Asia which influenced much of the Maritime Southeast Asia. The earliest solid proof of its existence dates from the 7th century; a Chinese monk, I-Tsing, wrote that he visited Srivijaya in 671 for 6 months. The first inscription in which the name Srivijaya appears also dates from the 7th century, namely the Kedukan Bukit Inscription around Palembang in Sumatra, dated 683.
Alexander	Alexander was tagus or despot of Pherae in Thessaly, and ruled from 369 BC to 358 BC. The accounts of his usurpation vary somewhat in minor points. Diodorus Siculus tells us that on the assassination of his father, the tyrant Jason of Pherae, in 370 BC, his brother Polydorus ruled for a year, and was then poisoned by Alexander, another brother. According to Xenophon, Polydorus was murdered by his brother Polyphron, and Polyphron, in 369 BC murdered by Alexander--his nephew, according to Plutarch, who relates also that Alexander worshiped the spear with which he slew his uncle as if it was a god.
Japan	Japan participated in World War I from 1914 to 1917, as one of the major Entente Powers and played an important role in securing the sea lanes in South Pacific and Indian Oceans against the Kaiserliche Marine. Politically, Japan seized the opportunity to expand its sphere of influence in China, and to gain recognition as a great power in postwar geopolitics.

Chapter 10. Central and Southern Asia, to 1400

Chapter 10. Central and Southern Asia, to 1400

On 7 August 1914, the Japanese government received an official request from the British government for assistance in destroying the German raiders of the Kaiserliche Marine in and around Chinese waters.

Chapter 11. East Asia, ca 800-1400

Funan	Funan was an ancient pre-Angkor Indianized kingdom located around the Mekong Delta. The ethno-linguistic nature of the people ; wether they were mostly Mon-Khmer or Austronesian, is the subject of much discussion among specialists. It is believed to have been established in the first century C.E. in the Mekong delta, which today is Vietnamese territory, although extensive human settlement in the region may have gone back as far as the 4th century B.C.E. Though regarded by Chinese envoys as a single unified empire, Funan may have been a collection of city-states that sometimes warred with one another and at other times constituted a political unity.
Japan	Japan participated in World War I from 1914 to 1917, as one of the major Entente Powers and played an important role in securing the sea lanes in South Pacific and Indian Oceans against the Kaiserliche Marine. Politically, Japan seized the opportunity to expand its sphere of influence in China, and to gain recognition as a great power in postwar geopolitics. On 7 August 1914, the Japanese government received an official request from the British government for assistance in destroying the German raiders of the Kaiserliche Marine in and around Chinese waters.
Song Dynasty	A: During the reign of the Song Dynasty the world population grew from about 250 million to approximately 330 million, a difference of 80 million. Please also see Medieval demography.
Tang Dynasty	The Tang Dynasty was an imperial dynasty of China preceded by the Sui Dynasty and followed by the Five Dynasties and Ten Kingdoms Period. It was founded by the Li (æ Ž) family, who seized power during the decline and collapse of the Sui Empire. The dynasty was interrupted briefly by the Second Zhou Dynasty (October 16, 690 - March 3, 705) when Empress Wu Zetian seized the throne, becoming the first and only Chinese empress regnant, ruling in her own right.
India	India, officially the Indian Empire, declared war on Germany in September 1939. The Provinces of India " href="/wiki/East_African_Campaign_(World_War_II)">East African Campaign, Western Desert Campaign and the Italian Campaign. At the height of the World War, more than 2.5 million Indian troops were fighting Axis forces around the globe.
Peasant	A Peasant is an agricultural worker who subsists by working a small plot of ground. The term Peasant today is sometimes used in a pejorative sense for impoverished farmers. Peasants typically make up the majority of the agricultural labour force in a Pre-industrial society, dependent on the cultivation of their land: without stockpiles of provisions they thrive or starve according to the most recent harvest.
Politics	Politics is a process by which groups of people make decisions. The term is generally applied to behavior within civil governments, but Politics has been observed in all human group interactions, including corporate, academic and religious institutions. It consists of "social relations involving authority or power" and refers to the regulation of a political unit, and to the methods and tactics used to formulate and apply policy.

Chapter 11. East Asia, ca 800-1400

Chapter 11. East Asia, ca 800-1400

Babylonia	Babylonia was a state in Lower Mesopotamia (Iraq), with Babylon as its capital. Babylonia emerged when Hammurabi (fl. ca. 1696 - 1654 BC, short chronology) created an empire out of the territories of the former kingdoms of Sumer and Akkad. The Amorites being a Semitic people, Babylonia adopted the written Semitic Akkadian language for official use, and retained the Sumerian language for religious use, which by that time was no longer a spoken language.
Roman	A Roman or civil diocese was one of the administrative divisions of the later Roman Empire, starting with the Tetrarchy. It formed the intermediate level of government, grouping several provinces and being in turn subordinated to a praetorian prefecture. The earliest use of "diocese" as an administrative unit was in the Greek-speaking East.
Silla	Silla (57 BC - 935 AD) (Korean pronunciation: [É•illa]) was one of the Three Kingdoms of Korea, and the longest sustained dynasty in Asian history. Although it was founded by King Park Hyeokgeose, who is also known to be the originator of the Korean family name Park (ë°•, æœ´), the dynasty was to see the Kyungju Kim (ê¹€, é‡') clan hold rule for most of its 992-year history. What began as a chiefdom in the Samhan confederacies, once allied with China, Silla eventually conquered the other two kingdoms, Baekje in 660 and Goguryeo in 668.
History	· History of the East Coast of the United States · History of the Southern United States · History of the United States · List of National Historic Landmarks in North Carolina · National Register of Historic Places listings in North Carolina
Regions	
Larger cities	
Smaller cities	
Major Towns	
Counties	
Aristocracy	Aristocracy is a form of government, in which a select few such as the most wise, strong or contributing citizens rule, often starting as a system of co-option where a council of prominent citizens add leading soldiers, merchants, land owners, priests, or lawyers to their number. Aristocracy deforms when it becomes hereditary elite. Aristocracies have most often been deformed to hereditary plutocratic systems.
Koinon	The Koinon (or "League") of Free Laconians was established in 21 BC by the Emperor Augustus, giving formal structure to a group of cities that had been associated for almost two centuries.

Chapter 11. East Asia, ca 800-1400

Chapter 11. East Asia, ca 800-1400

	The Eleutherolakones (á¼˜λευθερολῆκωνες, free Laconians) are first mentioned in 195 BC, after Sparta"s defeat in the Roman-Spartan War. The Roman general Titus Quinctius Flaminius placed several coastal cities of the Mani Peninsula under the protection of the Achean League, freeing them from Spartan hegemony.
Force	In physics, a Force is any external agent that causes a change in the motion of a free body, or that causes stress in a fixed body. It can also be described by intuitive concepts such as a push or pull that can cause an object with mass to change its velocity, i.e., to accelerate, or which can cause a flexible object to deform. Force has both magnitude and direction, making it a vector quantity.
Kamikaze	The Kamikaze) were suicide attacks by military aviators from the Empire of Japan against Allied naval vessels in the closing stages of the Pacific campaign of World War II, designed to destroy as many warships as possible. Kamikaze pilots would attempt to intentionally crash their aircraft - often laden with explosives, bombs, torpedoes and full fuel tanks - into Allied ships. The aircraft"s normal functions, to deliver torpedoes or bombs or shoot down other aircraft, were put aside, and the planes were converted to what were essentially manned missiles, in a desperate attempt to reap the benefits of greatly increased accuracy and payload over that of normal bombs.
Nigeria	Nigeria , officially the Federal Republic of Nigeria, is a federal constitutional republic comprising thirty-six states and one Federal Capital Territory. The country is located in West Africa and shares land borders with the Republic of Benin in the west, Chad and Cameroon in the east, and Niger in the north. Its coast lies on the Gulf of Guinea, a part of the Atlantic Ocean, in the south.
Empire	The term Empire derives from the Latin imperium. Politically, an Empire is a geographically extensive group of states and peoples united and ruled either by a monarch (emperor, empress) or an oligarchy. Geopolitically, the term Empire has denoted very different, territorially-extreme states -- at the strong end, the extensive Spanish Empire and the British Empire (19th c.), at the weak end, the Holy Roman Empire (8th c.-19th c), in its Medieval and early-modern forms, and the Byzantine Empire (15th c.), that was a direct continuation of the Roman Empire, that, in its final century of existence, was more a city-state than a territorial Empire.
Ottoman	The state of the Ottomans which began as part of the Anatolian Seljuk Sultanate and became an independent Empire, has been known historically by different names at different periods and in various languages. This page surveys the history of these names and their usage. · Modern Turkish: OsmanlÄ± BeyliÄŸi; The first declaration of statehood happened under Osman I. · Ä€l-e Uá¹мÄn

Chapter 11. East Asia, ca 800-1400

· Medieval Latin: Turchia
· Medieval Latin: Imperium Turcicum
· English: Turkey ; the current use of the name Turkey refers to the Republic of Turkey which succeeded the Ottoman Empire in 1923
· English: Turkish Empire, Ottoman Empire, Osmanic Empire, Osmanian Empire
· Ottoman Turkish/Persian: Ø¯ÙˆÙ„Øª Ø¹Ù„ÙŠÙ‡ Ø¹Ø«Ù…Ø§Ù†ÙŠÙ‡ Devlet-i Âliye-yi Osmâniyye
· Ottoman Turkish/Persian: Devlet-i Âliye (The Sublime State)
· Ottoman Turkish/Persian: Devlet-i Ebed-Müddet
· Ottoman Turkish/Persian: Memâlik-i Mahrûse (The Well-Protected Domains)
· Ottoman Turkish/Persian: Memâlik-i Mahrûse-i Osmanî
· Modern Turkish: OsmanlÄ± Ä°mparatorluÄŸu (Ottoman Empire),
· Arabic: Ø§Ù„Ø¯ÙˆÙ„Ø©Ù Ø§Ù„Ø¹Ù„ÙŠØ©Ù Ø§Ù„Ø¹Ø«Ù…Ø§Ù†ÙŠØ©Ù Ad-Dawlat al-Ë¤Ä€lÄ« al-Ë¤UthmÄ nÄ«
· Bulgarian: ĐžÑ Đ¼Đ°Đ½Ñ ĐºĐ° Đ¸Đ¼Đ¿ĐµÑ€Đ¸Ñ (Osmanska Imperia)
· Greek: ΟθωμανικÎ® ΑυτοκρατορÎ¯α
· Armenian: Õ•Õ½Õ´Õ¡Õ¶ÕµÕ¡Õ¶ Ô¿Õ¡ÕµÕ½Ö€Õ¸Ö‚Õ©ÕµÕ¸Ö‚Õ¶ (Osmanyan Kaysroutyoun)

In diplomatic circles, the Ottoman government was often referred to as the "Sublime Porte", a literal translation of the Ottoman Turkish Bâb-Ä± Âlî, which was the only gate of the imperial TopkapÄ± Palace that was open to foreigners, and where the Sultan, Grand Vizier or Viziers greeted the ambassadors.

Ottoman Empire

The Ottoman Empire or Ottoman State , also known by its contemporaries as the Turkish Empire or Turkey , was an empire that lasted from 1299 to November 1, 1922 (as an imperial monarchy) or July 24, 1923 (de jure, as a state.) It was succeeded by the Republic of Turkey, which was officially proclaimed on October 29, 1923.

At the height of its power (16th-17th century), it spanned three continents, controlling much of Southeastern Europe, Western Asia and North Africa.

Chapter 12. Europe in the Middle Ages

Empire

The term Empire derives from the Latin imperium. Politically, an Empire is a geographically extensive group of states and peoples united and ruled either by a monarch (emperor, empress) or an oligarchy. Geopolitically, the term Empire has denoted very different, territorially-extreme states -- at the strong end, the extensive Spanish Empire and the British Empire (19th c.), at the weak end, the Holy Roman Empire (8th c.-19th c.), in its Medieval and early-modern forms, and the Byzantine Empire (15th c.), that was a direct continuation of the Roman Empire, that, in its final century of existence, was more a city-state than a territorial Empire.

March

March Â·) is the third month of the year in the Gregorian Calendar, and one of the seven months which are 31 days long.
March in the Southern Hemisphere is the seasonal equivalent of September in the Northern Hemisphere.
The name of March comes from ancient Rome, when March was the first month of the year and named Martius after Mars, the Roman god of war.

Rome

Rome is the capital of Italy and the country"s largest and most populous city, with over 2.7 million residents in a municipality of some 1,285.3 km^2 (496.3 sq mi), while the population of the urban area is estimated by Eurostat to be 3.46 million. The metropolitan area of Rome is estimated by OECD to have a population of 3.7 million. It is located in the central-western portion of the Italian Peninsula, on the Tiber river.

Aristocracy

Aristocracy is a form of government, in which a select few such as the most wise, strong or contributing citizens rule, often starting as a system of co-option where a council of prominent citizens add leading soldiers, merchants, land owners, priests, or lawyers to their number. Aristocracy deforms when it becomes hereditary elite.
Aristocracies have most often been deformed to hereditary plutocratic systems.

Northumbria

Northumbria or Northhumbria was a medieval kingdom of the Angles, in what is now north-east England and southern Scotland, becoming subsequently an earldom in a united Anglo-Saxon kingdom of England. The name reflects the approximate southern limit to the kingdom"s territory: the Humber Estuary.
Northumbria was formed in central Great Britain in Anglo-Saxon times.

Peasant

A Peasant is an agricultural worker who subsists by working a small plot of ground. The term Peasant today is sometimes used in a pejorative sense for impoverished farmers.
Peasants typically make up the majority of the agricultural labour force in a Pre-industrial society, dependent on the cultivation of their land: without stockpiles of provisions they thrive or starve according to the most recent harvest.

France

France or ; French: [fÊ É·Ìfs]), officially the French Republic , is a country located in Western Europe, with several overseas islands and territories located on other continents. Metropolitan France extends from the Mediterranean Sea to the English Channel and the North Sea, and from the Rhine to the Atlantic Ocean. It is often referred to as L"Hexagone ("The Hexagon") because of the geometric shape of its territory.

Chapter 12. Europe in the Middle Ages

Chapter 12. Europe in the Middle Ages

Greenland	Greenland (Danish: Grønland; Kalaallisut: Kalaallit Nunaat, meaning "Land of the people") is an autonomous constituent country within the Kingdom of Denmark located between the Arctic and Atlantic Oceans, east of the Canadian Arctic Archipelago. Though physiographically a part of the continent of North America, Greenland has been politically associated with Europe (specifically Denmark) since the 18th century. In 1979, Denmark granted home rule to Greenland, with a relationship known in Danish as Rigsfællesskabet, and in 2008 Greenland voted to transfer more competencies to the local government.
Iceland	The Republic of Iceland () (Icelandic: Ísland; IPA: [Ë^islant]), is an island country located in the North Atlantic Ocean. It has a population of about 320,000 and a total area of 103,000 km^2. Its capital and largest city is Reykjavík, home to approximately 50% of the national population.
Imperialism	The term Imperialism commonly refers to a political or geographical domain such as the Ottoman Empire, the French Empire the Russian Empire, the Chinese Empire etc., but the term can equally be applied to domains of knowledge, beliefs, values and expertise, such as the empires of Christianity or Islam . Imperialism is usually autocratic, and also sometimes monolithic in character. Imperialism is found in the ancient histories of the Assyrian Empire, Chinese Empire, Roman Empire, Greece, the Persian Empire, and the Ottoman Empire , ancient Egypt, India, the Aztec empire, and a basic component to the conquests of Genghis Khan and other warlords.
Italy	Italy (Italian: Italia), officially the Italian Republic (Italian: Repubblica Italiana), is a country located on the Italian Peninsula in Southern Europe and on the two largest islands in the Mediterranean Sea, Sicily and Sardinia. Italy shares its northern, Alpine boundary with France, Switzerland, Austria and Slovenia. The independent states of San Marino and the Vatican City are enclaves within the Italian Peninsula, and Campione d"Italia is an Italian exclave in Switzerland.
Holy Roman Empire	The Holy Roman Empire) was a union of territories in Central Europe during the Middle Ages and the Early Modern period under a Holy Roman Emperor. The first emperor of the Holy Roman Empire was Otto I, crowned in 962. The last was Francis II, who abdicated and dissolved the Empire in 1806 during the Napoleonic Wars.
Pisa	Pisa was the name of an ancient town in the western Peloponnese, Greece. The area controlled by Pisa was called Pisatis, which included Olympia, the site of the Ancient Olympic Games. Pisa and Pisatis were subjugated by Elis in 572 BC. Currently, it is a village within the municipality of Olympia.
Roman	A Roman or civil diocese was one of the administrative divisions of the later Roman Empire, starting with the Tetrarchy. It formed the intermediate level of government, grouping several provinces and being in turn subordinated to a praetorian prefecture. The earliest use of "diocese" as an administrative unit was in the Greek-speaking East.

Chapter 12. Europe in the Middle Ages

Chapter 12. Europe in the Middle Ages

Fourth Crusade

The Fourth Crusade (1202-1204) was originally intended to conquer Muslim-controlled Jerusalem by means of an invasion through Egypt. Instead, in April 1204, the Crusaders of Western Europe invaded and conquered the Christian (Eastern Orthodox) city of Constantinople, capital of the Byzantine Empire. This is seen as one of the final acts in the Great Schism between the Eastern Orthodox Church and Roman Catholic Church.

Ottoman

The state of the Ottomans which began as part of the Anatolian Seljuk Sultanate and became an independent Empire, has been known historically by different names at different periods and in various languages. This page surveys the history of these names and their usage.

· Modern Turkish: OsmanlÄ± BeyliÄŸi;
The first declaration of statehood happened under Osman I.

· Ä€l-e Uá¹mÄ n

· Medieval Latin: Turchia
· Medieval Latin: Imperium Turcicum
· English: Turkey ; the current use of the name Turkey refers to the Republic of Turkey which succeeded the Ottoman Empire in 1923
· English: Turkish Empire, Ottoman Empire, Osmanic Empire, Osmanian Empire
· Ottoman Turkish/Persian: Ø¯ÙˆÙ„Øª Ø¹Ù„ÙŠÙ‡ Ø¹Ø«Ù…Ø§Ù†ÙŠÙ‡ Devlet-i Âliye-yi Osmânîyye
· Ottoman Turkish/Persian: Devlet-i Âliye (The Sublime State)
· Ottoman Turkish/Persian: Devlet-i Ebed-Müddet
· Ottoman Turkish/Persian: Memâlik-i Mahrûse (The Well-Protected Domains)
· Ottoman Turkish/Persian: Memâlik-i Mahrûse-i Osmanî
· Modern Turkish: OsmanlÄ± Ä°mparatorluÄŸu (Ottoman Empire),
· Arabic: Ø§Ù„Ø¯ÙˆÙ„Ø©Ù Ø§Ù„Ø¹Ù„ÙŠØ©Ù Ø§Ù„Ø¹Ø«Ù…Ø§Ù†ÙŠØ©Ù Ad-Dawlat al-ʿĀlīä al-ʿUthmānī«
· Bulgarian: Žž𝑅 Ð¼Ð°Ð½Ñ ка Ð¸Ð¼Ð¿ÐµÑ€Ð¸Ñ (Osmanska Imperia)
· Greek: Οθωμανικί® ΑυτοκρατορΓ α
· Armenian: Օ•Օ½Օ Օ¡Օ¶Օµօ¡Օ¶ Օ¿օ¡Օµօ½Օ€Ո ̧Ո©ՕµՕ ̧Ո¶ (Osmanyan Kaysroutyoun)
In diplomatic circles, the Ottoman government was often referred to as the "Sublime Porte", a literal translation of the Ottoman Turkish Bâb-Ä± Âlî, which was the only gate of the imperial TopkapÄ± Palace that was open to foreigners, and where the Sultan, Grand Vizier or Viziers greeted the ambassadors.

Japan

Japan participated in World War I from 1914 to 1917, as one of the major Entente Powers and played an important role in securing the sea lanes in South Pacific and Indian Oceans against the Kaiserliche Marine. Politically, Japan seized the opportunity to expand its sphere of influence in China, and to gain recognition as a great power in postwar geopolitics.
On 7 August 1914, the Japanese government received an official request from the British government for assistance in destroying the German raiders of the Kaiserliche Marine in and around Chinese waters.

Chapter 12. Europe in the Middle Ages

Chapter 12. Europe in the Middle Ages

Syria	Syria operated under a federalist system during its period of French rule . Its constituents were organized on primarily ethno-religious lines: there were separate states for Maronites, Alawites, Druze and Turks. The federal system was abolished after the Syrian independence in 1946.
Nigeria	Nigeria , officially the Federal Republic of Nigeria, is a federal constitutional republic comprising thirty-six states and one Federal Capital Territory. The country is located in West Africa and shares land borders with the Republic of Benin in the west, Chad and Cameroon in the east, and Niger in the north. Its coast lies on the Gulf of Guinea, a part of the Atlantic Ocean, in the south.
Portugal	Portugal , officially the Portuguese Republic (Portuguese: República Portuguesa), is a country on the Iberian Peninsula, member of the European Union and one of the founding members of NATO. Located in southwestern Europe, Portugal is the westernmost country of mainland Europe and is bordered by the Atlantic Ocean to the west and south and by Spain to the north and east. The Atlantic archipelagos of the Azores and Madeira are also part of Portugal. The land within the borders of today"s Portuguese Republic has been continuously settled since prehistoric times.
Reconquista	The Reconquista was a period of 800 years in the Middle Ages during which several Christian kingdoms of the Iberian Peninsula succeeded in retaking the Iberian Peninsula from the Muslims. The Islamic conquest of the Christian Visigothic kingdom in the eighth century extended over almost the entire peninsula (except major parts of Galicia, the Asturias, Cantabria and the Basque Country). By the thirteenth century all that remained was the Nasrid Kingdom of Granada, to be conquered in 1492, bringing the entire peninsula under Christian leadership.
Alexander	Alexander was tagus or despot of Pherae in Thessaly, and ruled from 369 BC to 358 BC. The accounts of his usurpation vary somewhat in minor points. Diodorus Siculus tells us that on the assassination of his father, the tyrant Jason of Pherae, in 370 BC, his brother Polydorus ruled for a year, and was then poisoned by Alexander, another brother. According to Xenophon, Polydorus was murdered by his brother Polyphron, and Polyphron, in 369 BC murdered by Alexander--his nephew, according to Plutarch, who relates also that Alexander worshiped the spear with which he slew his uncle as if it was a god.
Ethnicity	Ethnicity plays a prominent role in pornography. Distinct genres of pornography focus on performers of specific ethnic groups, or on the depiction of interracial sexual activity. Ethnic pornography typically employs ethnic and racial stereotypes in its depiction of performers.
India	India, officially the Indian Empire, declared war on Germany in September 1939. The Provinces of India " href="/wiki/East_African_Campaign_(World_War_II)">East African Campaign, Western Desert Campaign and the Italian Campaign. At the height of the World War, more than 2.5 million Indian troops were fighting Axis forces around the globe.

Chapter 12. Europe in the Middle Ages

Chapter 12. Europe in the Middle Ages

Law	The great end, for which men entered into society, was to secure their property. That right is preserved sacred and incommunicable in all instances, where it has not been taken away or abridged by some public Law for the good of the whole ... If no excuse can be found or produced, the silence of the books is an authority against the defendant, and the plaintiff must have judgment.
Swabia	Swabia, Suabia, or Svebia is both a historic and linguistic region in Germany. Swabia consists of much of the present-day state of Baden-Württemberg (specifically, historical Württemberg and the Hohenzollerische Lande, but not the western region of Baden), as well as the Bavarian administrative region of Swabia. In the Middle Ages, Baden, Vorarlberg, the modern principality of Liechtenstein, modern German-speaking Switzerland, and Alsace were also considered to be a part of Swabia.
Constitution	A Constitution is set of rules for government--often codified as a written document--that establishes principles of an autonomous political entity. In the case of countries, this term refers specifically to a national Constitution defining the fundamental political principles, and establishing the structure, procedures, powers and duties, of a government. By limiting the government"s own reach, most Constitutions guarantee certain rights to the people.
Constitutions	Bahrain has had two constitutions in its modern history. The first one was promulgated in 1973, and the second one in 2002. .
Factory	A Factory (previously manuFactory) or manufacturing plant is an industrial building where workers manufacture goods or supervise machines processing one product into another. Most modern factories have large warehouses or warehouse-like facilities that contain heavy equipment used for assembly line production. Typically, factories gather and concentrate resources: workers, capital and plant.
Koinon	The Koinon (or "League") of Free Laconians was established in 21 BC by the Emperor Augustus, giving formal structure to a group of cities that had been associated for almost two centuries. The Eleutherolakones (á¼"λευθερολÎ¬κωνες, free Laconians) are first mentioned in 195 BC, after Sparta"s defeat in the Roman-Spartan War. The Roman general Titus Quinctius Flaminius placed several coastal cities of the Mani Peninsula under the protection of the Achean League, freeing them from Spartan hegemony.
Ottoman Empire	The Ottoman Empire or Ottoman State , also known by its contemporaries as the Turkish Empire or Turkey , was an empire that lasted from 1299 to November 1, 1922 (as an imperial monarchy) or July 24, 1923 (de jure, as a state.) It was succeeded by the Republic of Turkey, which was officially proclaimed on October 29, 1923. At the height of its power (16th-17th century), it spanned three continents, controlling much of Southeastern Europe, Western Asia and North Africa.

Chapter 12. Europe in the Middle Ages

Chapter 12. Europe in the Middle Ages

Ottoman Turks	The Ottoman Turks were the subdivision of the Ottoman Muslim Millet that dominated the ruling class of the Ottoman Empire. Reliable information about the early history of the Ottomans is scarce. According to some sources (references needed), the leader (khan) of the Kayi tribe of the Oguz Turks, Ertugrul, left Persia in the mid-thirteenth century to escape the invading Mongols.
Spice trade	The Spice trade is a commercial activity of ancient origin which involves the merchandising of spices, incense, herbs, drugs and opium. Civilizations of Asia were involved in Spice trade from the ancient times, and the Greco-Roman world soon followed by trading along the Incense route and the Roman-India routes. The Roman-Indian routes were dependent upon techniques developed by the maritime trading power, Kingdom of Axum (ca 400s BC-AD 1000s) which had pioneered the Red Sea route before the 1st century.
Ice	Ice is a solid phase, usually crystalline, of a non-metallic substance that is liquid or gas at room temperature, such as carbon dioxide ice (dry ice), ammonia ice, or methane ice. However, the predominant use of the term ice is for water ice, technically restricted to one of the 15 known crystalline phases of water. In non-scientific contexts, the term usually means ice I_h, which is known to be the most abundant of these solid phases.
Oireachtas	From 1922 to 1937 the Oireachtas was the legislature of the Irish Free State. Until the final days of the Irish Free State it consisted of the King and two houses: Dáil Éireann and Seanad Éireann (also known as the "Senate"). Like the modern Oireachtas, the Free State legislature was dominated by the powerful, directly elected Dáil.
Rebellion	Rebellion is a refusal of obedience. It may, therefore, be seen as encompassing a range of behaviors from civil disobedience and mass nonviolent resistance, to violent and organized attempts to destroy an established authority such as the government. Those who participate in Rebellions are known as "rebels".
Antioch	Antioch on the Orontes was an ancient city on the eastern side of the Orontes River. It is near the modern city of Antakya, Turkey. Founded near the end of the 4th century BC by Seleucus I Nicator, one of Alexander the Great"s generals, Antioch eventually rivaled Alexandria as the chief city of the Near East and was a cradle of gentile Christianity.

Chapter 12. Europe in the Middle Ages

Chapter 12. Europe in the Middle Ages

History
- History of the East Coast of the United States
- History of the Southern United States
- History of the United States
- List of National Historic Landmarks in North Carolina
- National Register of Historic Places listings in North Carolina

Regions

Larger cities

Smaller cities

Major Towns

Counties

Combat

Combat is purposeful violent conflict intended to establish dominance over the opposition.
The term "Combat" typically refers to armed conflict between military forces in warfare, whereas the more general term "fighting" can refer to any violent conflict. Combat violence can be unilateral, whereas fighting implies at least a defensive reaction.

Chapter 12. Europe in the Middle Ages

Chapter 13. Civilizations of the Americas, ca 400-1500

Ethnicity	Ethnicity plays a prominent role in pornography. Distinct genres of pornography focus on performers of specific ethnic groups, or on the depiction of interracial sexual activity. Ethnic pornography typically employs ethnic and racial stereotypes in its depiction of performers.
Empire	The term Empire derives from the Latin imperium. Politically, an Empire is a geographically extensive group of states and peoples united and ruled either by a monarch (emperor, empress) or an oligarchy. Geopolitically, the term Empire has denoted very different, territorially-extreme states -- at the strong end, the extensive Spanish Empire and the British Empire (19th c)., at the weak end, the Holy Roman Empire (8th c.-19th c)., in its Medieval and early-modern forms, and the Byzantine Empire (15th c)., that was a direct continuation of the Roman Empire, that, in its final century of existence, was more a city-state than a territorial Empire.
Guatemala	Guatemala is a country in Central America bordered by Mexico to the north and west, the Pacific Ocean to the southwest, Belize to the northeast, the Caribbean to the east, and Honduras and El Salvador to the southeast. Its size is just under 110,000 km^2 with an estimated population of 14,000,000. A representative democracy, its capital is Guatemala City.
Honduras	Honduras is a republic in Central America. It was formerly known as Spanish Honduras to differentiate it from British Honduras . The country is bordered to the west by Guatemala, to the southwest by El Salvador, to the southeast by Nicaragua, to the south by the Pacific Ocean at the Gulf of Fonseca, and to the north by the Gulf of Honduras, a large inlet of the Caribbean Sea. Its size is just over 110,000 km^2 with an estimated population of almost 7,500,000.
Inca Empire	The Inca Empire (or Inka Empire) was the largest empire in pre-Columbian America. The administrative, political and military center of the empire was located in Cusco in modern-day Peru. The Inca Empire arose from the highlands of Peru sometime in early 13th century. From 1438 to 1533, the Incas used a variety of methods, from conquest to peaceful assimilation, to incorporate a large portion of western South America, centered on the Andean mountain ranges, including large parts of modern Ecuador, Peru, western and south central Bolivia, northwest Argentina, north and north-central Chile, and southern Colombia.
India	India, officially the Indian Empire, declared war on Germany in September 1939. The Provinces of India " href="/wiki/East_African_Campaign_(World_War_II)">East African Campaign, Western Desert Campaign and the Italian Campaign. At the height of the World War, more than 2.5 million Indian troops were fighting Axis forces around the globe.
Teotihuacan	Teotihuacan is an enormous archaeological site in the Basin of Mexico, containing some of the largest pyramidal structures built in the pre-Columbian Americas. Apart from the pyramidal structures, Teotihuacan is also known for its large residential complexes, the so-called "Avenue of the Dead", and numerous colorful, well-preserved murals. At its zenith in the first half of the 1st millennium CE, Teotihuacan was the largest city in the pre-Columbian Americas.

Chapter 13. Civilizations of the Americas, ca 400-1500

Chapter 13. Civilizations of the Americas, ca 400-1500

Roman	A Roman or civil diocese was one of the administrative divisions of the later Roman Empire, starting with the Tetrarchy. It formed the intermediate level of government, grouping several provinces and being in turn subordinated to a praetorian prefecture. The earliest use of "diocese" as an administrative unit was in the Greek-speaking East.
Tenochtitlan	Tenochtitlan (Classical Nahuatl: TenÅchtitlan [tenoË tÊʃËˆtitÉ¬an]) (sometimes paired with Mexico as Mexico Tenochtitlan or Tenochtitlan Mexico) was a Nahua altepetl (city-state) located on an island in Lake Texcoco, in the Valley of Mexico. Founded in 1325, it became the seat of the growing Aztec empire in the 15th Century, until captured by the Spanish in 1521. It subsequently became a cabecera of the Viceroyalty of New Spain, and today the ruins of Tenochtitlan are located in the central part of Mexico City.
Peru-Bolivian Confederation	The Peru-Bolivian Confederation (or Confederacy) was a short-lived confederated state that existed in South America between the years 1836 and 1839. Its first and only head of state, titled Supreme Protector, was the Bolivian president, Marshal Andrés de Santa Cruz. The Confederation was a loose union between the states of Peru (by this time divided into a Republic of North Peru and a Republic of South Peru, which included the capital Tacna) and Bolivia.
Iroquois	The Iroquois are an indigenous people of North America. In the 16th century or earlier, the Iroquois came together in an association known as the Iroquois League, or the "League of Peace and Power". The original Iroquois League was often known as the Five Nations, and comprised the Mohawk, Oneida, Onondaga, Cayuga, and Seneca nations. After the Tuscarora nation joined the League in the 18th century, the Iroquois have often been known as the Six Nations.
Peru	Peru , officially the Republic of Peru), is a country in western South America. It is bordered on the north by Ecuador and Colombia, on the east by Brazil, on the southeast by Bolivia, on the south by Chile, and on the west by the Pacific Ocean. Peruvian territory was home to the Norte Chico civilization, one of the oldest in the world, and to the Inca Empire, the largest state in Pre-Columbian America. The Spanish Empire conquered the region in the 16th century and established a Viceroyalty, which included most of its South American colonies. After achieving independence in 1821, Peru has undergone periods of political unrest and fiscal crisis as well as periods of stability and economic upswing.
Colombia	Colombia , officially the Republic of Colombia), is a constitutional republic in northwestern South America. Colombia is bordered to the east by Venezuela and Brazil; to the south by Ecuador and Peru; to the north by the Caribbean Sea; to the northwest by Panama; and to the west by the Pacific Ocean. Colombia also shares maritime borders with Jamaica, Haiti, the Dominican Republic, Honduras, Nicaragua and Costa Rica. Colombia is the 26th largest nation in the world and the fourth largest in South America. It has the 29th largest population in the world and the second largest in South America, after Brazil. Colombia has the third largest Spanish-speaking population in the world after Mexico and the United States.

Chapter 13. Civilizations of the Americas, ca 400-1500

Chapter 13. Civilizations of the Americas, ca 400-1500

Ecuador

Ecuador, officially the Republic of Ecuador, literally, "Republic of the equator") is a representative democratic republic in South America, bordered by Colombia on the north, Peru on the east and south, and by the Pacific Ocean to the west. It is one of only two countries in South America (with Chile) that do not have a border with Brazil. The country also includes the Galápagos Islands in the Pacific, about 965 kilometres (600 mi) west of the mainland.

Imperialism

The term Imperialism commonly refers to a political or geographical domain such as the Ottoman Empire, the French Empire the Russian Empire, the Chinese Empire etc., but the term can equally be applied to domains of knowledge, beliefs, values and expertise, such as the empires of Christianity or Islam . Imperialism is usually autocratic, and also sometimes monolithic in character.

Imperialism is found in the ancient histories of the Assyrian Empire, Chinese Empire, Roman Empire, Greece, the Persian Empire, and the Ottoman Empire , ancient Egypt, India, the Aztec empire, and a basic component to the conquests of Genghis Khan and other warlords.

Curaca

A Curaca was an official of the Inca Empire, who held the role of magistrate, about 4 levels down from the Sapa Inca, the head of the Empire. The Curacas were the heads of the ayllus (clan-like family units). They served as tax collector, and held religious authority, in that they mediated between the supernatural sphere and the mortal realm.

Rome

Rome is the capital of Italy and the country"s largest and most populous city, with over 2.7 million residents in a municipality of some 1,285.3 km^2 (496.3 sq mi), while the population of the urban area is estimated by Eurostat to be 3.46 million. The metropolitan area of Rome is estimated by OECD to have a population of 3.7 million. It is located in the central-western portion of the Italian Peninsula, on the Tiber river.

Chapter 13. Civilizations of the Americas, ca 400-1500